TEACHING SECONDARY
SCIENCE WITH ICT

Learning and Teaching with Information and Communications Technology

Series Editors: Tony Adams and Sue Brindley

The role of ICT in the curriculum is much more than simply a passing trend. It provides a real opportunity for teachers of all phases and subjects to rethink fundamental pedagogical issues alongside the approaches to learning that pupils need to apply in classrooms. In this way it foregrounds the ways in which teachers can match in school the opportunities for learning provided in home and community. The series is firmly rooted in practice and also explores the theoretical underpinning of the ways in which curriculum content and skills can be developed by the effective integration of ICT in schooling. It addresses the educational needs of the early years, the primary phase and secondary subject areas. The books are appropriate for pre-service teacher training and continuing professional development as well as for those pursuing higher degrees in education.

Published and forthcoming titles:

Adams & Brindley (eds): *Teaching Secondary English with ICT*
Barton (ed.): *Teaching Secondary Science with ICT*
Florian & Hegarty (eds): *ICT and Special Educational Needs*
Johnston-Wilder & Pimm (eds): *Teaching Secondary Maths with ICT*
Loveless & Dore (eds): *ICT in the Primary School*
Monteith (ed.): *Teaching Primary Literacy with ICT*
Monteith (ed.): *Teaching Secondary School Literacies with ICT*
Hayes & Whitebread (eds): *Supporting ICT in the Early Years*
Stern: *Teaching RE with ICT*
Way & Beardon (eds): *ICT and Primary Mathematics*

TEACHING SECONDARY
SCIENCE WITH ICT

Edited by
Roy Barton

Open University Press

Open University Press
McGraw-Hill Education
McGraw-Hill House
Shoppenhangers Road
Maidenhead
Berkshire
England
SL6 2QL

email: enquiries@openup.co.uk
world wide web: www.openup.co.uk

and Two Penn Plaza, New York, NY 10121-2289, USA

First published 2004

A catalogue record of this book is available from the British Library

ISBN 0 335 20862 2 (pb)   0 335 20863 0 (hb)

Library of Congress Cataloging-in-Publication Data
CIP data applied for

Typeset by RefineCatch Limited, Bungay, Suffolk
Printed in Great Britain by MPG Books Ltd, Bodmin, Cornwall

CONTENTS

List of contributors   vii
Series editors' preface   ix

Introduction   1
Roy Barton

Part I The School Context   **5**

1   Using ICT in a secondary science department   7
    Rob Musker

Part II Practical Science with Computers   **25**

2   Why use computers in practical science?   27
    Roy Barton

3   Management and organization of computer-aided practical work   40
    Roy Barton

4   Planning, teaching and assessment using computer-aided
    practical work   52
    Roy Barton and Caroline Still

Part III Using Information 69

5 Using the Internet in school science 71
Patrick Fullick

6 Multimedia in science teaching 87
Jerry Wellington

Part IV Interpreting Data 105

7 Handling and interpreting data in school science 107
John Wardle

Part V An International Perspective 127

8 The approach to ICT in science education in the Netherlands 129
Ton Ellermeijer

Part VI What Next? 137

9 Integrating ICT into science education and the future 139
Laurence Rogers

10 Closing remarks 155
Roy Barton

Index 159

LIST OF CONTRIBUTORS

Roy Barton, University of East Anglia. Before joining the university Roy spent 18 years as a secondary school science teacher, much of this time as head of physics in two comprehensive schools. His research interests are centred on the use of ICT for teaching and learning, particularly in science education and initial teacher education. He has produced many publications in both areas of study.

Ton Ellermeijer, AMSTEL Institute, University of Amsterdam. For many years Ton has been a leading figure in the development of ICT in science education in the Netherlands. He is particularly interested in the use of interactive video to support the teaching of physics.

Patrick Fullick, University of Southampton. Patrick has worked on curriculum development projects, including SATIS, Salter's Science and Cambridge Modular Sciences, and has written texts for GCSE and A-level sciences. He recently won an international award for *ScI-Journal*, an innovative project that publishes school students' science work on the Internet.

Robert Musker, Lancashire Grid for Learning. Robert was previously head of science at Archbishop Temple School, Preston. He is co-author of Heinemann's *ICT Activities for Science* and the *Eureka* series. His chapter relates to his experiences while teaching science at the Cornwallis School in Kent.

Laurence Rogers, University of Leicester. Formerly a school teacher of physics, electronics and science, Laurence has fostered research and curriculum development interests in the applications of ICT to teaching. He has been responsible for developing a range of hardware and software for science and technology education, his best-known works being *Motion Sensor* (1989), *Understanding Insight* (1998), *Control Insight* (2000) and *Insight 4* (2002).

Caroline Still, University of East Anglia. Before joining the university in 2000 Caroline spent 15 years as a secondary school science teacher. At the university she is involved in the initial training of science teachers and is currently responsible for the secondary science PGCE course. Her research interests centre on science education.

John Wardle, Sheffield Hallam University. John's background is in teaching science in secondary schools. He became an advisory teacher and later a project officer for NCET (now BECTa). More recently he has worked with the TTA on the ICT Training Needs Identification software and leading the Teaching and Learning Group in the Science Consortium, the only NOF-approved training provider to focus on science.

Jerry Wellington, University of Sheffield. Jerry's main area of research is in science education and the use of ICT in education. This has resulted in a wide range of publications, including five major books and 32 journal articles since 1980.

SERIES EDITORS' PREFACE

It would be unusual now in science to encounter students who do not use ICT in their school or leisure time, and equally unusual to encounter science teachers who do not incorporate ICT in some way into their teaching. However, this was not always the case. In the early days, it took a while for the dazzling ICT presentation effects to diminish in impact so that we could begin to think about using ICT as an integral part of making our teaching more effective, instead of just more visually interesting. But at this stage came the realization that in order to use ICT effectively, we had to begin to understand teaching and learning in greater depth. Developing science teaching with ICT is not, as Laurence Rogers reminds us in his chapter, simply about reversioning traditional science teaching, but 'invite[s] thinking about new opportunities for teaching and learning'. We see this type of thinking emerging in three major ways.

First is the place of science in a world that is rapidly becoming shaped by ICT use in both leisure and the workplace. Formal curriculum documents, such as the National Curriculum in the UK, recognize that science has a particular and significant relationship with technology, and one that affects the individual and society. The National Curriculum for science (p. 102) states:

> Through science, pupils understand how major scientific ideas contribute to technological change – impacting on industry, business and

medicine and improving quality of life . . . [Pupils] learn to question and discuss science-based issues that may affect their own lives, the direction of society and the future of the world.

The interplay between science and technology has a direct effect on the 'real world'. 'Improving quality of life' is rooted in the opportunities ICT brings through, for example, speed and automation. In the classroom, students can explore the wider world, gathering information about and evaluating events such as space travel through websites such as NASA. With ICT, we have the makings of global scientists who, through collaboration, can indeed affect 'the future of the world'.

Second, science is a subject where ideas are linked with practical investigation. Science requires demonstrable evidence of the validity of any theory. Part of teaching science is to bring about 'scientific thinking' in students: a mind set that requires students to test out, through experimentation, any given thesis. As Brendan O'Neill, Chief Executive of Imperial Chemicals Industry plc, observes: 'Studying science teaches us to be good at analysis and helps us to make complex things simple. It trains minds in a way that industry prizes.' Training minds is about bringing about scientific thinking, based on real and observable phenomena, tested through experimentation. In the classroom, much has changed in this field. Experiments once undertaken in the laboratory are now, with the rightly strict guidelines of health and safety, no longer permitted in a school setting. However, through the use of ICT, whether CD-ROM, PowerPoint presentation or websites, virtual demonstrations can continue, ensuring that science teachers can still use experimentation as a fundamental scientific process but, with the added facilities of provisionality and interactivity, can not only demonstrate experiments in safety but illustrate the dangers of incorrect procedures, thus enhancing the understanding of the scientific processes under investigation.

In biology, ICT has the same function for understanding how the body works. Dissection, again no longer seen in classrooms, can be undertaken virtually. Indeed, so effective is ICT in this area that teaching hospitals such as Addenbrooks at Cambridge now have virtual learning classes in anatomy for the students. Taking a walk around a liver is not an experience that students would ever have – but the benefits of understanding anatomy in this way are clear in the evaluations of the system given by both teaching staff and trainee medics.

Third, and importantly, science is about ideas. ICT, through all of its dimensions – speed and automation, provisionality, interactivity and capacity and range – can support the scientific imagination in exploring the 'what ifs' of scientific knowledge. As Professor Susan Greenfield says in the introduction to the science National Curriculum, 'Science is valuable because it meshes with all our lives and allows us to channel and use our spontaneous curiosity'. ICT allows the what ifs to become temporary realities, explorable in space and time in ways that pre-ICT days simply could not support.

In a subject with the breadth of the science curriculum, any volume can offer only a representation of the curriculum content. The pedagogies, ideas and processes explored in this volume belong to a range of areas within the science curriculum, but all the approaches explored here belong to the whole of science: to ways of representing the subject, to transferable ideas and strategies and to opportunities to break down barriers that have stood in the way of the scientific imagination in bringing about changes for the better in all our lives.

Tony Adams and Sue Brindley

INTRODUCTION

Roy Barton

The book is intended to identify and explore the ways in which ICT can be used to enhance secondary science education. While a predominately practical approach is taken, this is backed up by considering the broader educational issues which inform and underpin the approach. The material is presented from a teacher's perspective, discussing the rationale for the use of a range of ICT applications, but also considering practical issues such as the selection of resources, lesson planning and the impact of ICT on classroom organization. The aim is to enable the reader to make the most effective use of the ICT 'tools' available, complementing and developing the ICT requirements set out for teachers in England in the National Opportunities Funded training (NOF) (TTA 1999) and the 'New Standards' equivalent requirements for Initial Teacher Training (DfEE 2002). Therefore this book will be useful for anyone involved in science education, whatever their current level of expertise in the use of ICT, including practising science teachers, trainee teachers and their tutors and mentors.

In terms of structure, the book is divided into six parts, each one dealing with a different aspect of ICT in science education. Part I starts by considering the place of ICT in science, and leads on to an exploration of ICT use in the context of a secondary school science department. The next three parts deal with practical science with computers, using information and interpreting data. These chapters deal with some of the main ICT applications that can be used in science teaching. Part V aims to set the previous discussion into a wider context by considering the ways in which another country, the Netherlands, has developed its use of ICT in science education in parallel with the developments in England. Finally, the last part of the book pulls the ideas presented earlier in the book together and attempts to consider future developments in this area. Contributors to this book are all experienced users of ICT in science education and their work is well known and respected in this field.

Part I, dealing with ICT in the context of a school science department, is written by Rob Musker, who has also published curriculum support material for science teachers in using ICT activities in their teaching (see

Chapter 1). Whilst the science department described may not be an 'ordinary' department in terms of the level of ICT resources available, his chapter provides an insight into some of the opportunities to enhance science education in an 'ICT rich' environment. In this chapter Rob used his personal experience and the results of research conducted in the school to provide guidance on a range of issues, such as the role of ICT in improving literacy and numeracy skills and the ways in which pupils react to extensive use of ICT in science. A significant part of the chapter is devoted to providing guidance on how to go about planning for an increased use of ICT within a school science department.

Part II, on practical science with computers, is written by Roy Barton, who has a number of years' experience in using, researching and writing about the use of computers in practical science. Chapter 2 looks in detail at the rationale for using computer-aided practical work. This is done by illustrating the significant features and potential benefits of this approach, stressing the importance of teachers considering their personal philosophy of the use of practical work, as a important step in deciding whether computer-aided practical work will assist in meeting these aspirations. The author expresses the view that if science teachers first appreciate the potential benefits of computer-aided practical work then they are in a much better position to plan for its implementation in their teaching. Chapter 3 moves on from considering *why* we might want to use computer-aided practical work to *how* we might do it. Therefore, this chapter is concerned mainly with classroom management and organizational issues related to the use of data-logging equipment. In addition to considering the selection of equipment, the chapter identifies alternative ways in which computers can be used with different levels of resources available to the science teacher. In Chapter 4 the ideas on the rationale and practical implementation of computer-aided practical work are brought together and illustrated by three lesson case studies, which include detailed lesson plans.

Part III of the book deals with ICT-based information sources for science teaching, looking in particular at the use of the Internet and multimedia resources. Patrick Fullick is a leading figure in the development of the use of the Internet, particularly as a publishing medium for pupils and teachers. In his chapter looking at the use of the Internet in school science, he explores the various ways in which the Internet will impact on the ways in which we find, publish and communicate information. He also includes important information about the concept of 'acceptable use' in the context of young people using the Internet. Jerry Wellington has written extensively on the use of ICT in science education and is an acknowledged expert in the use of multimedia resources. In his chapter he provides a reflective and balanced discussion on the use of multimedia. He considers issues such as what is meant by authentic and inauthentic labour for pupils studying science and also explores the risks and opportunities of the use of multimedia in science teaching. The discussion is enriched by the inclusion of the views of teachers and pupils who have made use of this type of software.

In Part IV John Wardle, a high-profile figure in educating science teachers in the use of ICT, gives us the benefit of his extensive experience in the ways in which ICT can be used to assist in handling and interpreting information in school science. The aim of the chapter is to reflect on the overall rationale and potential benefits of ICT 'tools' such as spreadsheets and modelling software in assisting science teachers to meet their overall teaching objectives. The ideas are illustrated by the discussion of three scenarios that explore the potential of using the ICT-assisted approach to data handling.

The first four parts of the book deal exclusively with the use of ICT in English schools and so, to provide a wider context and as a means of evaluating an alternative approach, Ton Ellermeijer provides an overview of developments in the use of ICT in science education in the Netherlands. Ton is a leading figure in the use of ICT in science education in the Netherlands and so is in an ideal position to provide this discussion. The chapter gives a fascinating picture of the parallel developments occurring in the Netherlands, particularly their recent activities aimed at integrating the use of a range of software 'tools', such as multimedia applications and data-logging software, into an all-purpose activity-based teaching and learning environment, called 'Coach 5'.

The task of considering 'what next?' in the final part of the book falls quite rightly to Laurence Rogers, who has been actively pushing back the frontiers of how we think about using ICT in science education, particularly in terms of the development of data-logging software, for well over a decade. In this chapter we are able to benefit from Laurence Rogers's ability to step back and see the whole picture. He considers the future direction of ICT in science education. Experience would suggest that making predictions in the area of ICT is particularly risky but, drawing on his considerable first-hand experience, Rogers is able to identify likely trends in hardware and software development. However, perhaps the most significant issues are those related to the ways in which ICT may influence how teachers and pupils work in the future.

References

DfES (2002) *Qualifying to Teach: Professional Standards for Qualified Teacher Status and Requirements for Initial Teacher Training*. London: The Stationery Office.
TTA (1999) *The Use of ICT in Subject Teaching*. London: TTA Publications.

Part I

The School Context

1

USING ICT IN A SECONDARY SCIENCE DEPARTMENT

Rob Musker

In an ideal world

Given a high level of resources, how could ICT transform a practical science lesson? Consider this scenario. The teacher brainstorms the background science ideas behind the experimental work using an interactive whiteboard or Mimio. The work is saved as a web page or put into a shared file from the laboratory via a radio link to the network, so that the pupils can use it that night.

The pupils undertake the experiment using data-logging equipment and take digital pictures and a video of the results of their experiment. The pupils finish the experiment and have a quick discussion among themselves before linking, via a webcam, to another school in another part of the country to discuss their experiments further. The teacher plays back the images and data from earlier work to refresh and review the topic undertaken. The pupils go home and write up the experiment using an authoring tool or word processor incorporating sound files of their method, video and pictures of their experiment. They also incorporate graphs and an analysis of their results with the help of a spreadsheet program. During this process the pupils use resources from the Internet or link to copies of relevant CD-ROMs on the school's network to support their work. The finished experimental report can be mailed to the teacher or put in the shared homework folder waiting to be marked electronically. The above scenario can really happen at my school but not necessarily with all these features at the same time. But it is exciting and stimulating to work in this way for both teachers and students.

How can we work towards this approach to teaching science? This chapter aims to explore some of the ways in which the elements discussed above are currently used in a comprehensive school and the impact they are having on the work of the science department.

The Cornwallis School

Writing from the perspective of a practising science teacher at the Cornwallis School (an 11–18 technology college with approximately 1575 pupils, in Maidstone, Kent), I have rooted this chapter in my own classroom experiences, recognizing nevertheless that Cornwallis is unusually well resourced in terms of information technology. It has almost 200 laptops and over 190 desktop computers and is a regional centre for the National Opportunities Funded (NOF) ICT training for teachers, a mentor school for Microsoft and the first school in England to have a campus-wide wireless network.

In the science department of 17 teachers, there is access to a set of 20 laptop computers, and each laboratory has up to four desktop computers available. The class sizes never exceed 25, which makes it possible to have a ratio of two pupils per computer in the laboratories. The department has two half-sets of data-logging equipment giving similar pupil access. One set uses Acorn pocketbook computers with Data Harvest Sense and Control data-loggers, while the other makes use of laptop computers and Data Harvest Easylog data-loggers.

While the school and the science department are currently far from typical, they do provide an indication of the likely impact that an ICT-rich environment might have on the workings of a school science department. In most science departments there are a range of factors which can impede the use of ICT, such as access to computers, peripheral devices and, significantly, the knowledge to use them effectively. Other factors that have been suggested include the lack of suitable teaching materials (Tebbutt 2000). This chapter explores the potential benefits and the organizational and other departmental issues that arise when many of these barriers are removed.

ICT in the science curriculum

Communication is at the heart of all scientific activity and is itself a key aspect of science education. The term communication is being used in its widest sense to include not only speaking and writing but also TV, radio and video, all of which can be linked and controlled by a computer. The use of ICT enables the pupils to save time and provides clear and effective ways of presenting scientific information. Table 1.1 shows some of the ways in which ICT can be used to assist the process of communicating within science lessons.

Table 1.1 ICT tools to aid communication in science lessons

Software program	Activities
Microsoft Word	Experiment reports, writing frames, templates, drag and drop activities
Microsoft PowerPoint	Slide shows and simulations
Microsoft Excel	Labelling activities
Macromedia Flash	Animated simulations of experiments and scientific concepts
Microsoft Frontpage	Web pages
Macromedia Dreamweaver	Web pages
Matchware Mediator	Web pages
Hot Potatoes	Crosswords and cloze exercises
Microsoft Visio	Memory maps, timelines, flow charts of experiments and food chains, labelling activities
Various	E-mail and video conferencing

In addition, programs such as the ones cited enable pupils to give added depth to written reports by including a results graph, a digital image of the equipment or videos of an experiment. The pupils can include hyperlinks to related documents or websites, thus enhancing, rather than replacing, more conventional means of communicating ideas and information. For example, pupils who can access a video of their experiment have a visual aid that helps them to follow and review the experiment at home. This will help them to write their methods, see the results again and evaluate their work much more effectively.

As with other subjects, science is now charged with the development of basic skills such as numeracy and literacy, and here again ICT offers opportunities for extending the learning in many aspects of the conventional science curriculum. Spreadsheets can support pupils in calculating formulae or modelling numerical relationships; sliders and scroll bars, part of the Form toolbar in Microsoft Excel, allow pupils to ascertain the relationships between numbers and specify which formulae the relationship could refer to (see Figure 1.1).

ICT can help numeracy in other more subtle ways, such as using the zoom facility in graphing software as an aid to understanding scale factors. A range of the software features provided in many graphing packages can provide useful tools to assist pupils in this area of the curriculum. Pupils

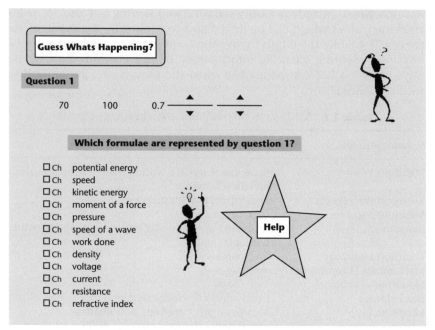

Figure 1.1 Use of scroll bars in Microsoft Excel

can often change instantaneously between different types of chart and graph to find the one that is more suitable for their data. In addition, the creative use of Microsoft Excel can produce spreadsheets and graphs that model pyramids of number looking at feeding relationships in ecosystems (the use of spreadsheets is discussed in more detail in Chapter 7).

ICT can also play an important part in supporting literacy work. Pupils writing about scientific concepts such as investigations, reports or work on historical ideas can be helped by using templates or writing frames, making the frames more (or less) explicit depending on the ability of the pupil. Supportive text provided by the teacher can be hidden on screen to stop it being printed out, allowing just the pupils' work to be seen. The example in Figure 1.2 shows how a letter template, using hidden text for prompts in Microsoft Word, can help pupils to structure their ideas about the developments Robert Hooke made on the light microscope.

Pupils can also use Microsoft PowerPoint to write presentations about historical characters and developments, incorporating sounds and even animations. Scientific spellings can be checked by pupils by using activities that use macros and conditional formatting in a product such as Excel, and at my school we have often found the pupils more confident and creative in their use of language with such support available to them.

Later in the book we will explore in detail the use of software that is

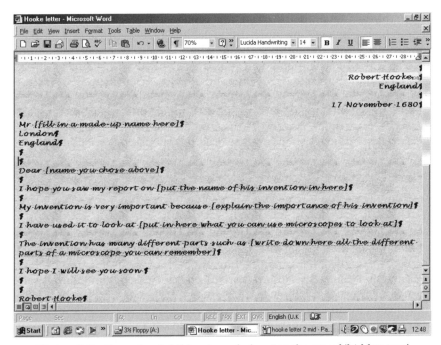

Figure 1.2   Example of children's work showing the use of 'hidden text' as prompts

particularly relevant to science teaching, such as data-logging software, information sources on CD-ROM and the Internet, and spreadsheet software. Clearly the use of these types of applications form the core of the ICT-related work within the science department. At this stage I want to provide an outline of the range of ways in which we have found ICT useful in science lessons.

Data-logging software is a particularly important application in science since it forms the interface between practical work and the use of ICT. Using and interpreting information from secondary sources are also important activities in science education. Common activities involve searching and using information from CD-ROM databases and the Internet. Other activities include using database software such as Information Workshop or Microsoft Access to create and interrogate databases on, for example, the planets of the Solar System, the periodic table or the classification of organisms. The information-handling activities I find most effective are Internet scavenger hunts and database activities on genetics data, such as 'Do tall people have big feet?' (Chapman *et al.* 2001). In this latter activity pupils look at continuous and discontinuous variation by making databases of their class results and using scatter graphs to study relationships between different physical attributes of the class. Therefore they can hypothesize about the relationships between the variables, for example in 'Do tall people have big feet?' measure the variables, analyse the data and draw conclusions easily using this software. There are also secondary data from another school so that pupils can compare their data with a larger sample.

Models allow pupils to change the variables in a scientific system and see their effects. Pupils start by learning how to manipulate simple models and progress to making their own. Simulations are often seen as a subset of this type of activity. Models themselves can also be broken into two groups: static models, such as those used for calculations such as an electricity bill, and dynamic models, which look at the changes within a system over a period of time (Carson 1997). There are many excellent commercial simulations currently available such as those in the New Medias Multimedia Science School, Maxis's SimLife and Crocodile Clips. SimLife provides a method of looking at food chains and evolution as the students can place different organisms on their own worlds and watch what happens to them very quickly over time. They can even invent their own organisms by amalgamating different parts of those already available. Multimedia Science School has many different types of simulations, ranging from those modelling particle theory and elements to those that model velocity and blood glucose levels.

Activities using spreadsheets such as Microsoft Excel have many more uses than just graphing and calculating formulae. For example, scientific images can be imported into Excel and labelled by inserting comments. Simulations, including the graphics, can be made using macros (a macro is a series of commands and functions that is stored in a Visual Basic module). They can be used to make activities that allow pupils to simulate the effects of different materials in blocking different types of radiation or the effect of changing the mass and distance of a planet on the gravitational pull of that planet. These activities allow students to experiment independently to find out how the relationships between the variables change. They are scientific concepts that pupils could not study by themselves or in practical situations.

Virtual learning

Over the past two years we have focused a great deal of energy evaluating different mechanisms for the delivery of online resources to support teaching at all Key Stages. As well as forming what we termed virtual classrooms on our own website, where resources for our courses could be downloaded, we have used several different 'portal systems' in a similar manner. The most common one used is Digitalbrain, often characterized as a virtual learning environment. Although the use of these within the classroom has not had an apparent significant impact yet on the achievement of the pupils at Key Stages 3 and 4 they have proved useful:

- in providing resources or extra homework to pupils in order to support their learning during their courses and at times when they need extra support, such as study leave and holidays;
- for e-mentoring of pupils through the portal's e-mail and chat forum facilities;
- to include all pupils in the learning process, even those who are ill or excluded;
- to organize ICT resources or science courses.

It is also apparent that these environments may have their greatest impact on those courses and subjects that have a large amount of assignment-based coursework, such as the applied science GCSE course. We are still evaluating other environments such as Microsoft's Encarta Class Server and Oracle's Think.com and we need to scale up our studies to see how truly effective these environments are.

ICT as a motivator

It is very difficult to pinpoint exactly how ICT improves the performance of pupils in tests. One problem when looking for a direct relationship between the use of ICT and pupils' performance in standard pencil-and-paper tests is that these tests are unlikely to relate directly to the skills being developed when using ICT. Assessment based largely on recall may well not reveal benefits in terms of improvements in conceptual understanding or the ability to analyse data more effectively. Considering the positive impact of ICT, one of the most important is probably due to an increased motivation for the subject (Musker *et al.* 1997). In science, visual aids, such as practical or video demonstrations, have always been used to explore difficult concepts and ICT can, especially in the form of simulations and models, greatly enhance the learning experience (NCET 1994a). It may be that the information presented in this way is put across in a different, more visually stimulating manner; for example, ICT also allows pupils to obtain results more quickly and easily and therefore allows them more time to interpret them. The results themselves, such as those from data-logging experiments, are more immediate and accurate. All these factors appeal to the pupils, especially the older ones.

Cornwallis is involved in using the materials produced as part of the Cognitive Acceleration through Science Education (CASE) programme, which emphasizes, among other things, the importance of classroom talk. Strong indications are that ICT can promote such discussion, enabling pupils to be more focused on their tasks and their discussion to be similarly focused. Simulations can be incorporated in 'CASE-like' activities to support the experimental parts of the lesson or in some cases instead of them. They should be used when they add an extra element to the lesson.

An example of this is density from explorescience.com. Students can study the effect of dropping shaped objects of different mass into a measuring cylinder to find their volume and on to a digital balance to find their mass. They can then drop them into a beaker to see if they float. The lesson can be structured to maximize the opportunities for pupils thinking but what takes this a step further is at that at a flick of a switch the density of the liquid used can be doubled or quadrupled. The objects rise to the surface and the students have to ponder why this happens. Discussion between pupils in lessons can also be encouraged using activities involving video clips in Microsoft PowerPoint or simple software animations using, for example, Macromedia Flash. The use of e-mail or video-conferencing means that these discussions or even those related to experiments or topic work do not have to be limited by the confines of the classroom (Musker 2000). In a project at my school called 'Mission to Mars', primary students video-conferenced with space research scientists at the Rutherford Appleton Laboratory after studying Moon rock and investigating how they could study the surfaces on the different planets.

At Cornwallis for over two years we have made use of a device called a Mimio, which when attached to an ordinary whiteboard enables everything drawn on the whiteboard to be displayed and saved on a computer. By using this device 'concept maps' can be created on the board, and each stage in building up the map can be saved to a computer (see Figure 1.3).

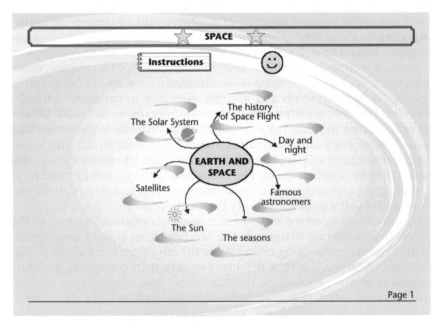

Figure 1.3   Visio space 'concept map'

Replaying this file enables the steps used to be revisited or even modified in the light of new understanding.

Pupils themselves appear to feel that ICT has a great impact on their performance. In a study at my school (Musker *et al.* 1997) the following reasons were given by pupils as to why computers made science more interesting, although it would seem that these comments could relate just as well to other curriculum areas:

- it allows me to work independently;
- it makes tasks quicker and easier ('I finish my work quicker when I use a computer');
- it is more entertaining than 'normal' lessons;
- it is more visual;
- it improves presentation (a response made only by boys).

Further findings showed us that over 85 per cent of the pupils surveyed enjoyed using computers in science lessons and almost all of these thought their use improved their understanding of science topics, although this was just based on the pupils' subjective judgement. The other 15 per cent of the sample did not enjoy using ICT in lessons. This group was predominantly made up of girls from lower band groups. These pupils stated that they preferred to have more traditional teacher-led lessons because these lessons needed fewer interactions from the pupils themselves (Musker *et al.* 1997). This would suggest that we need to reconsider how we introduce and support these pupils when using ICT. However, for the majority of pupils ICT has been found to allow flexibility for an individual's learning needs; for example, pupils can work at their own pace and go over work they are unsure of with a computer (NCET 1994a). The type of activity used in the classroom also has an effect on the enjoyment of the pupils. In the Musker study, activities involving PowerPoint, CD-ROMs and the Internet were considered by these pupils as being the most enjoyable. These activities rated highly as they allowed the pupils the opportunity to work independently and the activities were more visual and sometimes more entertaining. Many boys also stated that they liked Microsoft PowerPoint as it improved their presentation and they could make it 'look cool' (Musker 2000), which is useful since it impacts on the motivation of such pupils. The tasks that involved using spreadsheets were deemed the least enjoyable, with activities using sensors and other software packages being rated between these activities (Musker *et al.* 1997). All these findings have allowed us to plan and write our activities taking into consideration what aspects of ICT the pupils enjoy doing and what may be the most effective uses of ICT for them.

Organizing ICT in a science department

Responsibility for ICT within a science department is often given to those who have the greatest enthusiasm, such as the ICT coordinator, or left to the head of the department to organize. More democratic departments may spend time developing their ideas and plans as a group. Whatever the situation, it is important to consider the following issues:

- the development of the ICT skills in science lessons;
- the purchasing of relevant resources to meet the specific needs of the department;
- the management of those resources;
- technical support;
- staff and pupil competence;
- staff training;
- how to evaluate whether the developments have been a success.

The development of ICT in a department starts with the identification of the needs and aims for ICT. A development plan can be drawn up to outline the targets, the time-scale for these aims and how they are going to be implemented. Furthermore, the plan should consider all the bullet points listed above and these will have to fit in with the school's development plan for ICT and any ICT policies. The aims of the plan should also be prioritized (NCET 1994b). For example, it may be that developing data-logging in Key Stage 3 is a higher priority than developing it in Key Stage 4. I will now deal with each of these issues in turn within the context of the science curriculum.

Curriculum

ICT can be integrated into the majority of lessons but its use must be carefully monitored so that it is educationally justified. Initially the activities must be easy to implement and known to work. The type and number of activities chosen will depend on many of the considerations already highlighted, especially staff competence and resources. We have found it important that the activities chosen are written into the departmental schemes of work, to ensure there is sufficient time for their inclusion and so that pupils' use of ICT is properly planned and monitored. Many departments now use schemes such as *Eureka* or *Spotlight Science*, which have ICT integrated into their course work, or use courses such as *ICT Activities for Science 14–16* that provide step-by-step guides to implement a wide variety of ICT activities. Our department uses ICT activities from the *Eureka* scheme in conjunction with our own activities and some from other written sources, including *ICT Activities for*

Science 14–16. These are planned to give us good coverage of the science curriculum that enhances learning and provides the pupils with opportunities to implement many different types of activity. ICT is also used in those topics in which it is difficult to incorporate practical work.

The department may also be involved in covering some of the requirements of the National Curriculum for ICT. It is possible to cover all the Key Stage 3 requirements within the science department but generally science departments in schools are expected to implement the measuring part of the ICT curriculum, through, for example, the use of data-logging equipment. In my department some of the most common experiments are: measuring the velocity of a trolley using light gates; investigating the rate of photosynthesis using an oxygen sensor; and studying neutralization using a pH sensor.

Hardware

There are many ways of using hardware and software in order to enable ICT to support the teaching of science. The number of computers available is obviously the biggest influence on how these activities will be managed. If the science classrooms have only a single computer it can be used as a demonstration tool, especially if a large monitor or, better still, a data projector is available. Single computers can also be used for extension activities or as part of a 'circus' of practical activities. If network rooms are available then science can use these effectively for all ICT activities except data-logging.

In my school, laptops are used widely, with many half-class clusters available around the school. We are also lucky to be supported by a radio network, which allows us to access the network in any of the rooms. Radio networks are already proving a success in many schools, as they allow teachers to teach in their own rooms, improving their confidence and allowing them access to the resources they use every day. Pupils can access all their ICT work wherever they are in the school, even on the school field. This ensures that their work is always saved and is also accessible to the teacher.

Peripheral devices

There are many extra pieces of hardware or peripheral devices that can make the curriculum more exciting or easier to implement. Some peripheral devices are a must, such as printers. Most now have infra red capabilities, allowing computers such as laptops to send documents for printing via this link. Table 1.2 lists some of the available equipment that I have found extremely valuable in science teaching.

Table 1.2   Useful peripheral devices

Device	Importance
The multimedia data projector	The most vital piece of equipment I use in my laboratory is the data projector. This is the most used piece of equipment in our department. It makes CDs come to life and makes teaching aspects of ICT and science clearer and easier. Pupil presentations are greatly improved and multimedia Internet pages are riveting on a big screen. Both videos and flexicams can be plugged into many projectors, thus saving money on buying TVs.
Mimio/interactive white board	The Mimio makes my white board interactive for much less money than an interactive white board. Every pen stroke can be saved on to a computer and played back at a later date to review the work. I found it excellently employed for making mind maps and everything can be saved and put on to the web so that pupils can access the information later. Interactive white boards such as SMART boards or Promethean boards have similar properties and offer other features, such as screen cams.
Digital cameras	Pictures and videos of experiments can be taken and incorporated into experiments or presentations within minutes. This gives pupils direct visual access to experiments for review purposes and makes presentations highly entertaining.
Data-logging equipment	This is improving every year as the technology makes even greater leaps and bounds. The onset of radio-linked boxes and sensors should open up opportunities for even easier to implement experiments, especially when studying different environments.
Scanners	These are great to support presentation work and for scanning in written work for use on the Internet.

An example: using digital video

Digital video cameras are expensive and they need suitable software to allow films to be edited. However, whole-class activities can be undertaken with just one camera and one computer for editing. A digital video camera can be used in any classroom and outside and is very portable. My students can write, film and edit presentations in an hour's lesson. We have used it to film virtual dissections, make interactive periodic tables and create plays about global warming. It has formed an integral part of my 'ICT (Innovation, Creativity and Thinking) in Science' project. Digital video is also an excellent way of observing lessons and analysing thinking skill lessons.

Software

The most common software in schools is probably the Microsoft Office suite of programs. This is very versatile software and all the programs can be used very successfully in science. There is also specialist software, which is discussed in detail in later chapters. There is much now that is good value for money but obtaining site licences for some of this software can be extremely expensive and you have to be careful not to break the terms of your agreements. Roger Frost (1997) has produced this helpful list to consider. Does the software fit the needs of the department in terms of:

- the curriculum targets;
- the learners' needs;
- hardware capabilities;
- ease of use;
- cost?

And does it enhance the science curriculum?

Ideally you want the software to be cheap and easy to use, to suit the computers you have, to save time or make scientific concepts easier to visualize and to be generic so that it fulfils many roles. Software that easily fulfils all these criteria includes data-logging software such as Insight or DataHarvest's Sensing Science Laboratory. National conferences such as the ASE Annual Meeting and the BETT Show provide a good opportunity to discuss ICT needs with many different software and hardware suppliers.

When you are considering which software, support materials and hardware to invest in, the needs of the pupils should be considered. This will include consideration of:

- educational and motivational qualities of the resources;
- pupils' ICT capabilities;
- differentiation;
- grouping of the pupils.

We have found that the varied experience of Year 7 pupils means that using ICT early in this year is difficult. We have spent some time not only teaching ICT as a course in Year 7 but also spending a few lessons teaching the pupils how to use specialist software, such as the data-logging kit. As a result of liaison with some of our feeder primary schools we now teach pupils in Years 5 and 6 how to use data-logging sensors in science, in preparation for their work in Year 7. Science teachers visit the primary school for a few sessions of about two hours to introduce and use data-logging equipment with the primary pupils. The teacher works closely with the primary staff to ensure that the science covered is suitable for the level of pupil and to build the links between the school.

Support material

There is a wide range of articles, books and on-line resources available to help teachers develop schemes of work to integrate ICT into their teaching. Journals such as the ASE's *School Science Review* have articles on software, hardware and using ICT in the classroom. Websites such as SciShop, (www.scishop.org), another ASE initiative, provide numerous ICT resources to download. Some of the ICT and science courses, such as *IT Activities for Science 11–14* (Chapman and Lewis 1998) and *ICT Activities for Science 14–16* (Chapman *et al.* 1999), also provide step-by-step guides on how to use different types of software and hardware as well as differentiated activity sheets.

Technical support

Sustained problems with hardware or software can lead to a lack of staff confidence in its use and may deter staff from wanting to use it. Computers develop faults and ICT equipment needs to be updated from time to time. Without technical expertise or access to expertise, the use of ICT in the classroom could grind to a halt. In my school we are fortunate to have three full-time IT technicians to maintain our capabilities, but this has been a recent development. Sometimes the provider of the network or hardware provides the expertise, but access to this sort of help can be variable.

How to train staff and develop ICT skills within the department

ICT training should aim to give staff the skills for their needs. This should enable the teachers to implement the activities outlined in the schemes of work and ensure the targets in the development plan are met. There are distinct stages in this process, outlined in Table 1.3.

At my school we have found that external training sessions are useful to excite and supply information on new software and hardware, but general skills training can be done successfully as part of a regular INSET programme within the department. Skills training seems to be most successful when it is done at the time it is needed and using the equipment present within the department ('just-in-time' learning).

Table 1.3 The stages in training staff in a science department

Stage	Action
A Identify the needs and competencies of the teachers	The skills of the teachers are assessed. This is normally done by questioning the teachers. I have found it is better to ask teachers not only if they can use a piece of software but also break it down to key skills with that software.
B Plan the training	The type of training received by the teachers is decided. The training may need to look at: • how the curriculum is developed; • how to improve the ICT skills of the teachers. The training can be delivered: • externally to harness expertise elsewhere; • on a school or departmental basis; • by self-study such as using an online training resource; • as part of a course such as NOF training.
C Carry out the training	The teacher undergoes the training session or course and uses it to help them implement their lessons or develop their curriculum planning.
D Evaluate the success of the training	The targets of the training such as the implementation of lessons, the effects on teaching and learning or the development of the curriculum need to be assessed (NCET 1994b).

Health and safety

Health and safety issues related to IT equipment have received much coverage in the press over the past few years and there are several European Union directives regarding its use. Teachers have overall responsibility to ensure that IT equipment is used correctly and safely, to avoid eye strain, tendonitis, carpal tunnel syndrome, repetitive strain injury and even electrocution.

Review and evaluate your use of ICT

The use of ICT should be evaluated to see if the educational and curriculum targets have been met. It is important to evaluate use regularly and act on what you find. When I evaluate its use within our science department I try to ensure that any changes reflect:

• targets in the development plan;
• the introduction of new software and hardware;
• the best use of the current resources;
• the current competence of the science staff;
• changes in the ICT or science curriculum.

Recently, looking at the use of the Mimio and interactive whiteboards in the department, I realized that these pieces of equipment were having an impact on learning when they were being used, but they were generally underused. There were two main reasons for this: first, the staff had not had much training in their use; second, because of the way they are used they had not been fully written into schemes of work. Therefore, we are solving these problems and already this is having an impact. What is important is that the position is evaluated constantly.

It is difficult to evaluate targets such as the effects of ICT on learning. In previous studies we have used pre- and post-test strategies, pupil and teacher questionnaires, interviews, observations and value-added indicators. The easiest and most obvious piece of evidence would be the ICT and science grades reported at the end of Key Stage 3. The process of evaluation should also remove lessons that are unsuccessful and add others that incorporate any new software or hardware where appropriate. Teacher evaluation is still the primary method to assess ICT lessons in our department.

The future

It is important that ICT helps pupils to learn and provokes them to think about science and scientific concepts. We have had some success in linking ICT and critical thinking skills, a sort of 'thinking ICT' approach, and I see great potential in this area. Sometimes technology is used to support and enhance thinking skills lessons and sometimes thinking skills strategies are used to give structure to or 'frame' ICT lessons. We have used several different thinking skill strategies such as de Bono's Six Hats (De Bono 1985), CASE and Concept mapping and cartoons to provide structure to lessons (McGuiness 1999). Related to this is the impact that ICT can have on science education outside the classroom. Pupils now have access to some high-quality science resources, such as simulations and revision material, at home and the teacher must be aware of the opportunities they offer and try to harness them if possible. The speed of technological change continues, with the key software and hardware making huge strides every year. The present generation of Microsoft Office products allows voice recognition and it will be interesting to see whether this can impact on how pupils record activities such as science investigations. Science teachers need to concentrate on the educational value of the software and hardware. We have found that by using these tools in an innovative way we have been able to enhance our lessons while retaining the main focus on learning science.

References

Carson, S. R. (1997) The use of spreadsheets in science – an overview, *School Science Review*, 79 (287): 69–80.

Chapman, C. and Lewis, J. (1998) *IT Activities for Science 11–14*. Oxford: Heinemann.

Chapman, C., Lewis, J., Musker, R. and Nicholson, D. (1999) *ICT Activities for Science 14–16*. Oxford: Heinemann.

Chapman, C., Musker, R., Nicholson, D. and Sheehan, M. (2001) *Eureka: Success in Science Activity Pack*. Oxford: Heinemann.

De Bono, E. (1985) *Six Thinking Hats*. New York: Little Brown.

Frost, R. (1997) Computer software for science teaching – choosing and using, *School Science Review*, 79(287): 19–24.

McGuiness, C. (1999) *From Thinking Skills to Thinking Schools*. London: DfEE.

Musker, R., Reardon, K., Poole, P. and Hearne, P. R. (1997) *The Enhancement of Academic Performance Due to an Enriched IT Curriculum*. London: Teacher Training Agency.

Musker, R. (2000) *The Effects of ICT on Learning in Science*. Torun, Poland: University Nicolas Copernika.

NCET (1994a) *IT Works: Stimulate to Educate*. Coventry: NCET.

NCET (1994b) *Enhancing Science with IT: Planning for IT*. Coventry: NCET.

Tebbutt, M. (2000) ICT in science: problems, possibilities . . . and principles? *School Science Review*, 81(297): 57–64.

Part II

Practical Science
with Computers

2

WHY USE COMPUTERS IN PRACTICAL SCIENCE?

Roy Barton

Introduction

I feel I should start this chapter by stating clearly that I am a strong advocate for the use of computer-aided practical work in science. My convic-
tion comes mainly from my experiences as a secondary school science
teacher. From the time of my own initial training, being inducted into the
possibilities of the Nuffield approach to science teaching, I felt that practical work had the potential greatly to enhance pupils' learning in science.
Although I never changed that view, over the years I became increasingly
frustrated by the logistical limitations on what could be done in the school
laboratory. I wanted pupils to spend more of their time analysing and
interpreting data but instead the exercise of collecting and processing the
data seemed to dominate. Consequently, in the late 1980s, when I first
became aware of the potential of computers to transform practical work, I
became a convert. In the account that follows I explain my reasons for this
'conversion'.

This part of the book looks at computer-aided practical work in three
chapters. This chapter is intended to provide a rationale for using computers. Chapter 3 looks at resources and other implications for the school
laboratory. In Chapter 4, three case studies provide specific examples

of how the ideas presented in the preceding two chapters could be put into practice. The sequence of these three chapters is significant, since it is my view that unless science teachers become convinced of the educational benefits of computer-aided practical work, there is no point in exploring such details as resources or activities. Science teachers need to be convinced at an intellectual, rather than just a practical, level that the educational benefits outweigh the problems, and realistically there are problems. My own experience, however, and that of colleagues, seems to indicate that once science teachers decide that they want to use computers for educational reasons, then they are adept at overcoming any organizational and logistical problems that may arise. A useful parallel is to consider the use of practical work itself. I think all science teachers would agree that it would be easier not to do practical work, since it gives rise to a range of logistical and classroom management-related difficulties. However, we continue to use practical work because the educational benefits outweigh the practical and financial problems. My argument is that the advantages of practical work become even more evident when we make use of *computer-aided* practical work. This is why this chapter argues in terms of educational advantage, while the following chapters deal with issues such as equipment and classroom organization.

Practical work

It is impossible to separate the aims of practical work in general from those related to computer-aided practical work. So it is useful to begin by exploring some fundamental questions about practical work; then we can sensibly explore what computers might offer in this area. In countries like Britain, where practical work has such a central place in science education, there is a danger of taking it for granted and not stepping back to consider why we devote so much of our time and limited resources to it. Interestingly, however, even a brief look at the very extensive literature on practical work in school science indicates that there is no clear consensus about why we are doing it and what the main objectives should be. One of the main areas of contention is the debate about the relative merits of illustrative and investigative practical work. Illustrative practical work is used to demonstrate a facet of science and pupils are usually guided by a series of step-by-step instructions, whereas investigative practical work stems from pupils' statements and predictions in response to what they have seen, experienced or discussed with the teacher. Whether you advocate one approach over the other, or even support a balance between the two approaches, I suggest that there is a subset of common goals for practical work, which most science teachers are likely to subscribe to. These include:

- encouraging pupils to become actively involved in science lessons, making them more likely to engage with the ideas and processes;
- providing pupils with a context in which to discuss their own ideas and to hear the ideas of others;
- providing pupils with the opportunity to suggest explanations for what they observe;
- providing pupils with the opportunity to try out their own ideas.

Equally important is the role of the teacher both during and after the activity. When pupils are engaged in practical work they need guidance, structure and most significantly an explanation of the context in which they are working. For example, after illustrative practical work, pupils need to be offered explanations, models and analogies from the teacher to help them in their efforts to construct their own understanding of what they have experienced. Following pupil-led investigations the teacher is also needed; for example, in helping pupils to identify ways in which they could improve areas such as planning, data analysis and identifying ways of improving future investigations. However, factors such as involvement, discussion and explanation, which have been identified above, are all present during conventional practical activities, so what is so special about using a computer?

Computer-aided practical work

Computer-aided practical work is conducted by collecting data using sensors connected to a data logger. This information is then transferred to a computer and displayed, usually in a graphical form, on a computer screen. The process is controlled by software (see Chapter 3 for more about this process), but in this chapter I wish to concentrate on teaching and learning issues. The first factor I would like to highlight relates to the ways in which the presentation of data on the computer screen has the potential to focus pupils' attention on the important process of analysis rather than on routine data processing. To illustrate this point I will use the example of a simple activity looking at cooling by evaporation. This can be done by using three temperature sensors (thermometers). One thermometer is placed on the desk as a control, while the others are dipped into a volatile liquid. Once the logging of data has started the two thermometers are removed from the liquid, and one is held still while the other is gently waved through the air. The data-logging software enables the temperature of each thermometer to be recorded as a graphical trace on the screen of a computer. A typical trace is shown in Figure 2.1.

By only seeing a static image of the final graph printed on the page we lose much of the benefit of the activity, but we can start to identify the advantages of this approach by considering the conventional alternative.

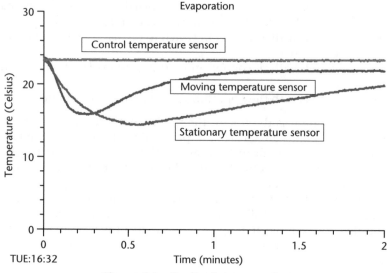

Figure 2.1   Cooling by evaporation

If it was possible to read a liquid-in-glass thermometer during an experiment of this type, pupils would focus entirely on the data collection during the activity. They would then be asked to 'plot a graph', and the subset who managed to do this successfully would at this stage be able to analyse the results. Contrast this with the approach outlined above, which has a number of advantages, including:

- providing an immediate link between the activity and the result, making it much more likely that the pupil will relate the graphical representation of the data to the activity itself;
- giving time for the pupil to think and to watch rather than being preoccupied by data gathering;
- making it possible to start with a qualitative analysis, which enables pupils to look at the overall shape of the graph in terms of the trends and gradients (the conventional approach requires pupils to deal with numbers in order to plot the graph before they can conduct a qualitative analysis);
- by seeing the data presented so quickly pupils are encouraged to ask 'what if?' questions and consequently to conduct follow-up activities;
- having the graph on the computer screen provides a focus for both pupils and the teacher to discuss the activity.

So is there a relationship between these advantages and the subset of aims for practical work identified earlier? Discussion of ideas, both the pupils' own and those of others, would be generated in a lively manner given the immediacy of the data presentation and the way in which the screen provides a central focus. The focus effect of the screen is also relevant when considering opportunities for providing explanations, both from the pupil and by the teacher. The ways in which this relates to the active involvement of pupils are perhaps more contentious. Many teachers have suggested to me that they are concerned that when using computer-aided practical work pupils will be relegated to mere bystanders. This is an important point worthy of further exploration.

Comparison of computer-aided and conventional approaches

During practical activity there are two ways to distinguish between the conventional and computer-aided approaches: the mode of measurement and the recording of data. In the case of measurement using the computer, data collection occurs automatically, whereas in the conventional approach, pupils need to read scales manually. Even though some may argue that pupils get a better 'feel' for the data if they read the scales, it is clear that a misreading of scales can introduce problems when it comes to pupils interpreting their data. Is the purpose of the activity to improve pupils' skills in reading a specific scale or is it more important to get good-quality measurements quickly so that pupils can move on to evaluate them? Clearly the answer to this question will not always be the same, but I would suggest that in most cases good-quality data are most significant. Manual recording is not only another potential source of errors; it also seems to have the effect of making pupils detached from the experiment itself. I have observed the ways in which manual data recording can become an end in itself (Barton 1996). Pupils seemed to 'switch off' during this time, taking on specific roles of reading or recording data, with no apparent thought for the meaning or significance of the values they were measuring. It should be noted that while the sensors are collecting the data in the computer-aided approach, the experiment is still taking place in front of the pupils on the laboratory bench. For example, when a gas syringe is being used with a position sensor to monitor the rate of a reaction, the pupils are still able to observe the evolution of gas as they have always done. Indeed, it could be argued that when pupils are freed from routine data gathering they are in an even better position to observe these events during the experiment, with the additional benefit of being able to relate them to the graphical representation appearing on the computer screen.

This leads on to the area of graphical analysis. Not only does the computer take over the task of data gathering, the software also frees pupils from the need to plot the graphs for themselves. There are arguments for and against this way of working. My view is that in science, graph plotting is simply a means to an end; we plot graphs to help us to interpret data.

In school science, presenting information in a graphical form is the cornerstone of our attempts to link data obtained during practical work with the abstract ideas and concepts of science. Until quite recently there was only one graphing option available if pupils had collected the data for themselves: the production of a manually plotted graph. However, we now have the computer option, although it may be fair to say that some science teachers still have reservations about automating graph plotting, feeling that the pupils will lose something in the process. However, as I hope to demonstrate, there are considerable advantages in using ICT in graphing.

So what do we know about computer-aided graphing? To explore this question I carried out some school-based research comparing the performance of pupils using computer-generated graphs with that of those plotting the same data manually. It is not appropriate to give extensive details of the research here but it involved Year 10 and Year 8 (15- and 13-year-old pupils) working in pairs, analysing electrical characteristic graphs, for components such as bulbs and resistors (Barton 1997). The main findings were:

- Pupils spent between three and four times longer producing graphs manually than when using the computer.
- Manual graph plotting was a problem for all, but particularly for the least able pupils. Errors in scale selection, plotting and choice of line tend to go uncorrected by pupils, which is a problem in the subsequent analysis.
- Best-fit lines are a particular problem in manual plotting.
- Manual plotting places an additional burden on pupils, since they need to identify the best-fit line before moving on to interpret the meaning of the graph they have plotted.

I am sure these findings will not surprise anyone who has taught science. However, I feel this 'additional burden' of manual plotting is particularly significant. Once individual points have been plotted it is sometimes possible for a range of alternative lines to be legitimately drawn through the points. This choice may well be influenced by prior experiences, such as the expectation that the data will form a straight line. It could be argued that manual plotting places an additional and unproductive burden on pupils, since they are required to try to set aside their preconceived ideas in order to plot the best-fit line before they move on to interpret the meaning of the graph they have plotted. Pupils using the computer are equally likely to expect straight line relationships but they have the benefit of seeing the graph produced on the computer screen before moving on to try to interpret the shape of the graph.

Although in this study there were no obvious differences between the groups in their ability to interpret graphs, the ways in which they approached this activity were different. Those using manual plotting tended to emphasize individual data items rather than the continuous nature of the relationship between the variables, with comments along the lines of 'because 1 is 0.16 and 2 is 0.23 and they are roughly sort of . . .' Those using the computer were much more likely to talk about the overall shape of the graphs, for example 'It curved more than I expected'. Consequently, I have become convinced that computer-aided graphing is not simply a time saver: there are distinct learning advantages for pupils. Finally, it is worth noting that pupils' descriptions of graphs were much more effective when they were dealing with two or more graphs on the same axes, a situation that is much more likely to occur when using computer-generated graphs.

Where does this leave manual graph plotting? In my view, it should be avoided if the *analysis* of data is the prime reason for producing the graph, as is the case for the majority of practical work. Producing a graph manually is unlikely to develop learning skills in science, the major focus for us as science teachers. If it is felt that the ability to construct a graph manually is an important life skill, then it should be taught using activities designed specifically for the purpose.

Demonstrating using computers

So far the discussion has centred on pupils conducting practical work in small groups, and now I consider computer-aided practical demonstrations. Demonstrations are an important part of science education, even, on occasion, providing spectacular and memorable events for pupils (and even occasionally teachers). Trying to involve pupils in the demonstration is particularly important and I feel that the real-time presentation of data when using a computer is significant in this respect. This option has been further enhanced by the onoing reductions in the price of data projectors, providing a convenient and effective means of displaying the computer screen for the whole class to see. Comments, questions and suggestions can all be made while the whole class is able to see the data emerge. Many effects – for example, using temperature probes – can be demonstrated within a couple of minutes. This gives the teacher the opportunity to encourage pupils to interpret the data collected and also to predict the effects of changes to the experimental conditions. Asking pupils to make sketch graph predictions is a good way of encouraging them to engage with the data; this approach becomes particularly effective when used with computers, since prediction and data collection are not separated by large gaps in time. To illustrate this approach I use the example of the 'coffee problem'. Imagine that you make a cup of coffee, and before you have chance to add the milk the telephone rings. Do you add the milk before you take the call or at the end, if you enjoy hot coffee? To explore this the temperature of two cups of hot water can be monitored, with cold water to be added to one cup at the start and the same amount of cold liquid to the other half way through the cooling time. We can ask pupils to draw sketch graphs of temperature against time for the two traces. This prediction can then be compared to the results collected by using a computer. If a data projector is used to project the screen on to a whiteboard, the predicted sketch graph can be drawn on to the whiteboard, as a collaborative effort of the whole class. The data collected by the computer can then be overlaid on to this sketch. Encouraging pupils to make predictions that can then be quickly tested is an effective way of increasing their involvement in the activity.

New opportunities when using computer-aided practical work

So far I have looked at the potential value added of computer-aided practical work compared with the conventional alternative. However, another significant area relates to what might be described as access to 'new' data. By this I mean measurements that are either not practical or simply not possible by conventional means. These 'new' measurements include: using a pH meter that enables continuous monitoring of pH; the ability simultaneously to monitor quantities such as the brightness of a filament bulb and the current flowing through it; and the ability to plot derived quantities such as the acceleration of an object as a function of its displacement from a fixed point. Some of these added benefits are derived by selecting combinations of sensors, as in the case of the filament bulb experiment, but others involve manipulating the computer software; for example, to define quantities derived from the measurements recorded by the sensors. Illustrative of this point is an experiment that can be used when studying insulation to extend the activity beyond simply measuring the rate of cooling. This involves using a heat flow sensor, which measures the rate of energy transfer through it directly in watts per square metre. The experiment involves monitoring the energy transfer from hot water placed in three stacked polystyrene cups. Two temperature probes are used to measure the temperature gradient by placing one in the hot liquid and the other between the outer two cups. The rate of energy transfer is measured by placing a heat flow sensor between the inner two cups. An example of the data collected by monitoring the two temperatures and the rate of energy transfer is shown in Figure 2.2.

Clearly the first benefit of this approach is access to the 'new' data of rate of energy transfer. However, the software also enables pupils to explore the relationship between the variables still further; for example, by defining a fourth quantity, the difference between the two temperature values. This enables pupils to compare rate of cooling directly with the temperature difference, as shown in Figure 2.3.

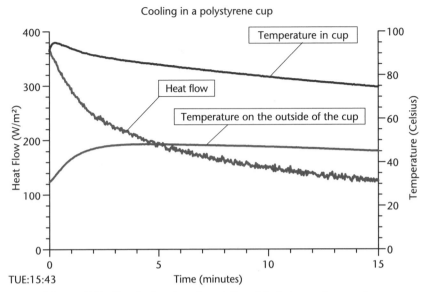

Figure 2.2 Graph showing the relationship between temperature measurements and the rate of energy transfer

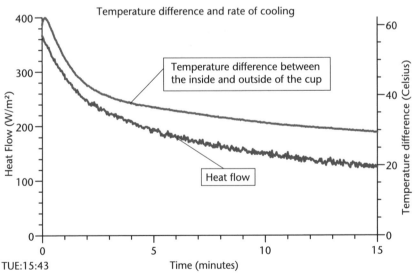

Figure 2.3 Graph comparing the rate of energy transfer and temperature difference

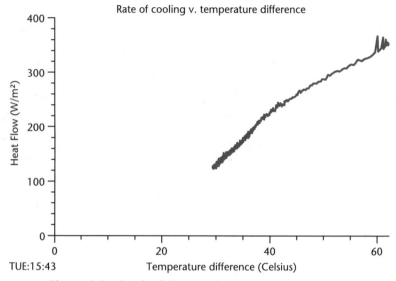

Figure 2.4   Graph of the rate of energy transferred against
temperature difference

The value added can go one stage further since the software can then be
set up to plot these variables against each other; that is, an *XY* plot as
opposed to a *YT* plot, as shown in Figure 2.4. Discussion of the significance
of the data presented in this graph would enable the key ideas of the
relationship between the temperature gradient and the rate of cooling to
be explored. I would argue that this example illustrates the potential of
accessing 'new' data via sensors such as the heat flow, together with ways
in which the software facilitates the manipulation of these data when
exploring the relationship between variables.

From the previous example it is clear that the software can provide a
powerful means of manipulating and presenting data. However, the analysing tools that are also available greatly assist this process, making the
graph the starting point for analysis rather than the end point. These tools
include, among others, the ability to obtain the ratio between any two
items of data or the value of the area under the graph, or to compare
quickly the gradients for two sets of data.

A further limitation of conventional practical work is that since data are
collected manually, experiments are usually confined to the arbitrary
length of a lesson and within the laboratory itself. However, data loggers
can function away from a computer and can operate using their
own internal power supply (for more information see Chapter 3). 'Remote
logging' gives pupils and teachers access to data that originate outside
the school laboratory. It is possible to conduct experiments that last several days, releasing the computer for other users during this time. This

greater flexibility increases the opportunities for pupils to engage in open-ended project work and it also provides more scope for pupil-designed investigations. Pupils are often more motivated to analyse data collected in this way, since they are 'their' data. Two of the case studies in Chapter 4 provide examples of the ways in which pupil-led investigations and remote logging can be conducted using computer-aided practical work.

The role of the teacher

The final area to discuss is the impact that computer-aided practical work has on the role of the teacher. At the start of this chapter I commented on the frustration I experienced as a science teacher at having to spend too much of the valuable lesson time in supporting pupils as they collected and processed information. I always felt that pupils would learn the concepts and ideas more effectively if there was more opportunity for them to talk about their ideas with the teacher and if there was more time for the teacher to provide the 'bridge' between their experiences during practical work and the abstract concepts they related to. These ideas of promoting discussion to aid the learning process are consistent with the constructivist approach to learning. The psychologist Vygotsky (1978) stressed the importance of language in cognitive development and Edwards and Mercer (1993) have argued that both action and discourse have a role to play. Driver *et al.* (1994) have also suggested that the construction of scientific knowledge involves both individual and social processes. All these arguments support the idea that discussion is an important element in learning science. I would argue that since computer-aided practical work increases all the types of discussion identified above, its use is consistent with these theories of how to promote learning.

In what ways can science teachers best exploit the opportunities for increased discussion offered by computer-aided practical work? Science teachers will need to focus much more on probing pupils' understanding and interpretation of the data on the screen. This is much more likely to occur, since in most cases the data will be available as the teacher moves around the room. The evidence from my own research suggests that pupils benefit from the experience of providing a verbal description of graphs. Rogers (1995), discussing the possibilities offered by data-logging, has provided what might be called a vocabulary of graphing that could be used as part of this process. It would seem that discussions between pupils and the teacher, facilitated by the computer-based method, could support pupils to become more effective in describing graphical data, and hence in analysing the results of their experiments. It would seem that the ideas of 'the guided construction of knowledge' suggested by Mercer (1995: 1) is greatly assisted when pupils discuss their ideas with teachers during computer-aided practical work.

Finally, we need to consider the impact of using computers on what we ask pupils to do during practical lessons. Using conventional methods pupils are often kept busy by the routine tasks identified earlier, and if nothing is put in their place when using data loggers pupils will occupy their time in unproductive ways. Therefore, teachers will need to devise new activities that exploit the rapid presentation of data in a graphical form. These can include the use of sketch graphs both to predict the data being collected and to consider the results of changing some of the original conditions. These sketch graphs can also be used as a means of recording the data on the screen, since it is often the overall shape of the graph that is important. This could be supplemented, if necessary, by asking pupils to record significant items of data, which has the advantage of avoiding long queues at the printer. We could also ask pupils to spend more time recording in a variety of ways their understanding of the data they have collected. I feel that prompt questions can be an effective way of focusing pupils' attention on this, often neglected, aspect of the experiment. Activities of this sort provide the opportunity for pupils to prepare and present their results to the rest of the class, which is another way in which the use of computer-aided practical work can promote discussion and replace data processing.

Conclusion

When I first became interested in using computers to support practical work in science I felt that it would simply involve replacing some experiments and introducing activities not possible before. However, over the years I have become aware of the pedagogical shifts that are needed in the activities we ask pupils to engage in and the ways in which the science teachers need to interact with pupils during the practical activity. These involve a much more interactive style of teaching that focuses much more on discussing ideas and the analysis of data than on supporting pupils as they collect and process results. Working with a small group of pupils with the central focus on the computer screen puts the teacher in a more dynamic and less controlled environment. These changes are difficult to implement and we all need time to adjust to these new roles. Therefore, I return to my original contention that teachers must be convinced on an intellectual level of the educational benefits that are possible, since to reap the benefits they will need to change their teaching approach to practical work.

I conclude with a few questions for you to consider. I have already made my views on the use of computer-aided practical work very clear, so you will not be surprised that these questions are somewhat loaded. However, I believe they are relevant for any science teacher who is in the process of deciding whether data-logging is worth the effort.

- Do pupils think about science during the collection of conventional data?
- Are pupils more likely to discuss an investigation if they have the focus of a computer screen showing the data collected?
- Do we want pupils to spend most of their time processing data or analysing data?
- Are pupils better able to interpret graphs if they plot them manually?
- Does the presentation of data on the computer screen, particularly in graphical form, improve pupils' ability to interpret the data?
- To what extent are less able pupils able to take part in the analysis of data if they are no longer required to plot graphs for themselves?

Much has changed since I first started to consider the impact of computers on practical work and it is now clear that in order to realize the full benefits of this approach there must be shifts in teaching approach and style. However, I remain convinced of the potential of this approach and I am sure that we have yet to feel the full impact of the possibilities it offers to enhance science education.

References

Barton, R. (1996) Computers and practical work in science education, Unpublished PhD thesis, University of East Anglia.

Barton, R. (1997) How do computers affect graphical interpretation?, *School Science Review*, 79(287): 55–60.

Driver, R., Asoko, H., Leach, J., Mortimer, E. and Scott, P. (1994) Constructing scientific knowledge in the classroom, *Educational Researcher*, 23(7): 5–12.

Edwards, D. and Mercer, N. (1993) *Common Knowledge: The Development of Understanding in the Classroom*. London: Routledge.

Mercer, N. (1995) *The Guided Construction of Knowledge: Talk amongst Teachers and Learners*. Clevedon: Multilingual Matters.

Rogers, L. T. (1995) The computer as an aid for exploring graphs, *School Science Review*, 76(276): 31–9.

Vygotsky, L. S. (1978) *Mind in Society: The Development of Higher Psychological Processes*. Cambridge, MA: Harvard University Press.

3

MANAGEMENT AND ORGANIZATION OF COMPUTER-AIDED PRACTICAL WORK

Roy Barton

Introduction

Chapter 2 was concerned with issues related to the potential teaching and learning benefits of computer-aided practical work. This chapter considers some of the practical and logistical considerations facing science teachers when making use of computers in this way. As I argued in Chapter 2, it is important that science teachers are able to establish for themselves a clear rationale in terms of potential educational benefits before considering the practical details discussed in this chapter.

The collection of data with the aid of sensors and computers, as part of practical work in science, started to be introduced into schools in the mid-1980s. In Britain, this activity is often referred to as data logging. I feel that this term is rather unhelpful, since it emphasizes simply the collection of data rather than the way in which the whole process of practical work is enhanced; hence I prefer to use the term computer-aided practical work when discussing the activity conducted by pupils and teachers and to reserve the term data logging for the equipment used in the process. A basic data-logging system involves sensors, an interface or data logger and a computer program.

The system works by the sensors responding to the physical quantities to be measured, such as temperature, light level or oxygen concentration, and converting these measurements into an electrical signal. This information is then passed by the interface or data logger to be displayed on the computer screen. In Britain the term interface is usually reserved for a device that is unable to store data, whereas a data logger has a built-in memory and so has the option of operating away from the computer. Seeing data presented as they are collected is referred to as 'real-time' logging, whereas using a data logger to collect information away from a computer is called 'remote' logging. Whichever method is used, after having been sent to a computer the information is often displayed on the computer screen in the form of a graph. The next section looks at the selection of equipment to support computer-aided practical work, followed by a discussion of the alternative ways of organizing practical work with computers.

Selection of equipment

The first option facing schools when selecting equipment to support computer-aided practical work relates to the choice between real-time only loggers or those that can operate both as real-time and remote loggers. Real-time loggers only work when connected to a computer and many of the advantages suggested for computer-aided practical work are gained when using the loggers in this way.

Data loggers that can operate away from a computer give the option of both modes of use but are more expensive. It is now standard for this type of equipment to support 'sensor recognition', which means that when a new sensor is connected to the logger the software will automatically identify it and its operating range, for example as a temperature sensor reading from $-10°C$ to $+110°C$. This is usually the case for both remote and real-time only loggers.

Most of the latest data loggers come with a built-in simple screen display. This makes it easy to set up the logger and is particularly useful for checking on data collection while logging remotely. The option to record one-off or 'snapshot' measurements rather than use continuous logging – for example, to sample the range of light levels in different habitats – is also a feature available on some loggers.

Remote logging can be set up in two ways. Most systems allow logging to be initiated away from a computer, which is possible because the sensors are recognized automatically due to the 'sensor recognition' discussed above. Since the time of the experiment has not been specified, the logger initially records data at its maximum rate until its memory is almost full; it then deletes every second data item, compacts the remaining data and continues at half the original logging rate. This allows loggers to record over many days independently of a computer. Since remote logging will be done using the internal battery power, it is worth identifying the length of time the logger can operate in this way. Battery life is usually extended when logging over a long period of time by using an internal clock that powers up the sensors only when measurements are being taken. The alternative to this 'plug in and go' approach is to set up the conditions for the experiment on the computer screen, specifying the sensors to be used, the length of time for the experiment and the way in which the data will be displayed. It is also possible to set up a condition that will initiate the logging; for example, when the light level falls below a certain value or by simply pressing a 'start' switch. Once this has been done the software can be used to 'download' this information to the logger.

Once the data have been collected they can be 'uploaded' to a host computer. Remote logging has the advantage that it can extend practical activities beyond the school laboratory (for example, into woods and sea shores) and also allows experiments to last for longer than a single science lesson. (One of the case studies presented in the next chapter explores how remote logging can support the biology curriculum by investigating water pollution.) At the other end of the scale some loggers have the facility to log data very rapidly, giving access to transient events, which are particularly useful in some physics applications.

Practical considerations

Since sensors are made to fit with particular logging systems they need to be considered at the same time as the decision on which data logger to purchase. When selecting sensors the two main factors to consider are their cost and how robust they are. The issue of cost is particularly important, since a science department is likely to spend more money on its range of sensors than in buying the data loggers themselves. Related to how robust the sensors are, it is also worth considering how easily they can be used in the particular experiment; for example, is the temperature sensor lead long enough to prevent the logger being too close to the experiment? Perhaps the final factor is the range of different types of sensors available, but competition between manufacturers usually means that most provide the main sensors you would wish to use.

Equally important is the decision about the software to be used. You need to be aware that your initial requirements are likely to be very different from those in the medium term. You will also need to decide whether to buy the software sold by the manufacturer of the logger or whether to buy third party software. Looking back at the discussion in Chapter 2 it is important to note that it is via the software that the majority of the classroom interaction occurs. In the short term you need to be convinced that the software is easy to use and that you will not need to relearn how to use it each time. However, you should also be planning to build on pupils' experience over time so that they can then use some of the more advanced features. Therefore, your software should ideally facilitate a progression in the level of sophistication in its use. Once pupils, and perhaps more importantly teachers, have become familiar with one software application it is more productive to extend what they can do with it rather than to start again with a new and more advanced application. Upgraded versions of software appear periodically; however, this is not the same as 'starting again'.

Computer-aided practical work is different from most other ICT applications, since we need to site the computers in the laboratory. The main factors here are the provision of sufficient computers and the space they occupy on crowded laboratory benches. Few schools are currently able to provide a laboratory with one computer between two pupils, a common group size for practical work. However, it is useful to note that it is not always necessary to use high-specification computers to conduct computer-aided practical work, so that science departments can effectively be opportunistic in recycling older computers in the school that are not fast enough for other ICT applications, such as the use of CD-ROMs or connection to the Internet. Unfortunately, desktop computers are not ideally suited for use in a school laboratory, since they take up large amounts of laboratory space and are difficult to move and store. A significant recent development has been the growing availability of affordable portable computers, recently with the added advantage of high-quality colour displays. These computers have a number of advantages for data logging over desktop computers. For example, they can be distributed and stored easily and they have a small 'footprint' on limited laboratory bench space. It is worth noting that relatively low-specification portable computers are suitable for computer-aided practical work.

School factors

Evidence from a number of schools suggests that the most effective way forward in integrating ICT into science teaching is to start with a very limited use of computers and slowly to extend and expand your use as pupils and teachers become more confident and competent. However, it is also vital that these activities become integral to the schemes of work used in the department. Perhaps it is useful to use the development of pupils' investigative skills as an analogy. It is sensible to start with limited but clear objectives when pupils are first introduced to conducting investigations. However, it is also important to plan for progression and for this planning to be written into the scheme of work. This careful planning ensures that pupils have the knowledge and skills to be able to make the next step in development. Finally, in the light of experience these ideas will need to be reviewed and adjusted. I would recommend this step-by-step approach as one that is likely to be much more sustainable than the 'big bang' approach of introducing whole-class data logging at a stroke. To illustrate this approach, later in the chapter I discuss some of the alternative ways of using different levels of data-logging equipment, alongside more conventional approaches.

Decisions about data-logging equipment are complex and depend on a number of factors. I have grouped these under three headings and identified some of the questions that need to be addressed.

Initial planning
- What funds are available, in the short and medium term?
- Is the development of data logging seen as a short- or long-term priority?
- What current data-logging equipment is available and is it sensible to add to it or should it be replaced?

Purchase of equipment
- Is the initial focus on real-time or remote logging, or do you require both?
- Is the intention to start with a limited number of loggers or is whole-class practical work seen as a priority?
- Is it a priority to have a whole-class display of the computer screen?

School and departmental issues
- What is the current ICT expertise and experience in the department?
- What level of priority is to be given to the development of computer-aided practical work by the department?
- How will the necessary training be provided (and funded)?
- What are the implications for technical support?
- What are the likely running costs for the department?
- What is the school's approach to the delivery of the National Curriculum for ICT?

Clearly there are so many factors identified above that it is not possible to discuss every possibility, so I will try to illustrate some of the issues by looking at one possible hypothetical scenario. This science department has a couple of data loggers in a cupboard, bought about five years ago by a previous head of department. Most science staff would rather not bother using computers in their lessons but the school's last Ofsted report said that this was a priority area and consequently the school has made some money available.

In these circumstances it would be counterproductive to consider making major alterations to the schemes of work and forcing staff into making immediate changes to their current practice. Identifying short-term goals that are achievable and having a clear well thought through longer-term plan is not only likely to be acceptable to Ofsted but, more importantly, much more likely to be successful in the longer term. In this case I would seriously consider starting again with new equipment. Initially, my main priority would be to buy equipment that enables teachers to conduct effective demonstrations using a high-quality data logger. This means that the first purchase would be a data logger with built-in display, a high-specification portable computer capable of making use of good-quality Internet access and a data projector. A data projector is a device that can be used to project a large image of a computer screen for the whole class to see. The significant features are that the device is small and portable and the images produced are sharp and bright. They have the added advantage that they can also be used to project images from video or DVD players, thereby replacing the need for bulky TV sets in the lab. Although still quite expensive, currently at slightly more than the cost of a single computer, they are in the process of revolutionizing the ways in which teachers are able to make use of a wide range of ICT applications. There is clear evidence that sustainable developments in the classroom use of ICT occur when teachers have free access to portable computers.

A set of sensors would be needed to complete the demonstration kit. It is important to buy a range of sensors that facilitate the kinds of measurements conducted in biology, chemistry and physics, being guided by examples drawn from the many publications giving ideas for data-logging experiments (Birrell 1996a, b; Watt 1996; Frost 1998).

Once a department has this demonstration facility, the remaining money should go towards a number of starter kits of data loggers and sets of sensors. It is probably sensible to buy a mixture of real-time only loggers and loggers capable of working remotely, making sure that the sensors will work on both types. I would only use recycled desktop computers as a short-term measure, if at all, preferring to equip the department progressively with portable computers. However, for pupil use only low-specification computers will be required.

The issue of staff training and development needs to be considered at the same time as the decision on the purchasing policy. Usually a mixture of in-house and external courses is the most productive but the cost implications need to be considered at this planning stage. Peer support and the informal exchange of ideas within the department is often the most effective form of in-service training. When considering training issues it is important to include the science technicians. They need to become familiar with the operation of the hardware and software and of course become familiar with the practical problems that will inevitably arise.

Science departments, particularly when provided with one-off injections of money, often do not consider the issue of running costs. Although it is difficult to get accurate figures it is clear that science departments on the whole seriously underestimate the costs of ICT maintenance, repair and replacement.

Alternative modes of use

Some schools have not developed their use of computer-aided practical work because they are not in a position to purchase a full class set of data-logging equipment. There are two reasons why this may not be a sensible approach to take. First, it is possible to conduct some effective computer-aided practical work making use of very limited resources; second, as discussed earlier, a phased introduction of the use of data-logging equipment provides the opportunity for staff and pupils gradually to develop and extend their abilities to use the equipment.

To explore just some of the range of the alternative ways in which teachers can make effective use of computer-aided practical work, I will focus particularly on examples involving the use of a small number of loggers.

Demonstration

Well-presented demonstrations are in themselves an effective teaching tool but when used in conjunction with data logging they become even more powerful. Real-time graphing can be used to bring out teaching points and is particularly powerful when teachers ask pupils to make predicted sketch graphs before the data are collected. However, it is important either to demonstrate experiments lasting a short time or to involve pupils in predicting what the trace will be when showing stored files of data. Clearly this is an option that is available even if the science department has only one data logger.

The option of using demonstrations is particularly appropriate for experiments involving expensive and less robust sensors, but again it is important to look for 'value added' in the use of the computer. I feel that all these criteria are met in the example whose data are graphed in Figure 3.1, which involves monitoring oxygen, humidity and temperature inside a bell jar containing a burning candle. This is a good example of where a sketch graph prediction prior to the collection of data would be a useful approach, particularly since many pupils are likely to predict that the oxygen level will fall to 0 per cent before the candle goes out. This is obviously an extension of a familiar experiment but the use of the sensors enables teachers to make much clearer links to ideas about combustion.

An extension of this idea relates to revision sessions. Again this is based around the use of a single data logger connected to a data projector. If a data logger has been used throughout the teaching of a particular topic, either by pupils or by the teacher, then it is possible to save a number of files that represent work done at different stages of the topic. This enables the teacher to enliven the session by illustrating the main points by referring to data collected at the time, but also provides the opportunity to collect new data as part of the revision exercise.

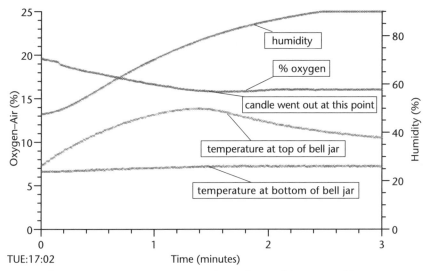

Figure 3.1   Monitoring oxygen, humidity and the top and bottom
temperatures inside a bell jar as a candle burns

Using data loggers alongside conventional equipment

If the school has more than one set of equipment but does not have
enough for a whole-class activity there are a number of options available.
For example, it is possible for either the teacher or a number of the pupils
to collect data using a data logger, while the rest of the class use the conventional equipment. An important advantage of this approach is that
plots of the data are available before the end of the lesson and can be used
to discuss the scientific ideas involved without waiting for the pupils to
produce a manual plot. It also provides a useful context in which to discuss
the relative advantages and disadvantages of computer-aided practical
work compared to the convention approach.

An example of where this would be appropriate would be when looking
at cooling curves and discussing latent heat. A typical graph of the data for
stearic acid and water is shown in Figure 3.2.

The possibility of completing the lesson with the whole group being
able to see the cooling curve graph can enable the teacher to try to
establish much clearer links between the data and the related scientific concepts. Pupils could be asked to sketch the graphs into their
book and be given a number of questions aimed at exploring and
developing their understanding. To illustrate this, consider how the
homework could be changed from the usual graph plotting exercise.

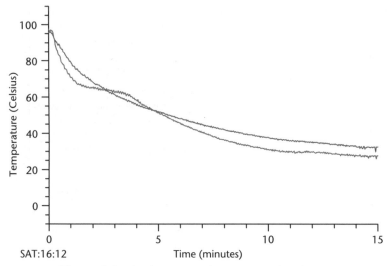

Figure 3.2 Cooling curves for stearic acid and water

For example,

- by asking pupils to label the graphs indicating the melting point;
- questions about changes in the movement and arrangement of the molecules represented by different parts of the sketch graph;
- drawing sketch graphs if the substances were heated from room temperature or if the cooling liquids were placed in a freezer at −20°C.

Such questions illustrate the ways in which the focus can be shifted from data processing to exploring pupils' understanding.

Circus of experiments

If you wish to give pupils hands-on experience in using data loggers but have only one set of equipment, one option is to use it as part of a circus of experiments. The use of a circus of experiments is a common approach with conventional equipment. It usually involves a number of different practical activities set out round the room, with the pupils working on each one in turn. It is often used when we want the pupils to experience a wide range of activities that do not take long to conduct. Clearly it would be possible to include one or more activities involving data logging within the 'circus', depending on the number available. This would be a good way of giving pupils their first 'hands-on' experience with data logging. It also has the advantage that the whole lesson does not depend on the equipment working and so it is less stressful if the teacher is new to data logging (however, managing a circus is not without its own stresses). An example of this approach would be a circus of short experiments on heating. In this case a data logger could be used to explore the absorption of radiation. The added value here, apart from the opportunity for pupils to use the equipment, is that the temperature traces enable you to discuss the different equilibrium temperatures while energy is being transferred to the surfaces, and the ways in which they cool once the energy source has been removed.

A 'dip-in-and-out' lesson

This is similar to the circus but the main focus of class activity in this case is a non-practical activity. During the lesson different groups use the computer for a short time. Once they have collected and printed their data another group can take their place. This is a good option if the school has only two, three or four data loggers available. Again, having the data logging less central to the lesson is a good way to make a start in using data logging in your teaching. The activities would need to be short, like the radiation experiment described above, but in any case computer-aided practical work takes much less time than the conventional alternatives. In this situation it would be easy for pupils to use a printer to get a copy of their results, avoiding the queues that sometime occur during whole-class practical work.

A 'half-and-half' lesson

If there are enough computers for about half the class to carry out a practical activity then you could use a 'half-and-half' lesson. In this case, half the class conducts a computer-aided practical activity, while the other half is given another non-computer-based exercise; for example, using conventional practical equipment or a text-based exercise. Half way though the lesson the groups swap over. This approach needs careful planning and timing, and is not recommended until you feel reasonably confident in using computers in your laboratory. Experiments involving exploring rates of reaction are activities that could be approached in this way. One of the case studies described in the next chapter also uses this approach to classroom organization. The data shown in Figure 3.3 were obtained by using the overlay function in the software, which allows the data collected in two separate experiments to be compared directly. Trace A had a concentration of 0.06 mol of sodium thiosulphate per dm^3 and trace B 0.12 mol/dm^3.

This is a good example of where the graph is the starting point for discussion, enabling questions such as: How long did the reaction take to start? When does the reaction finish? How does the reaction rate change? Where should we measure the rate of reaction? It provides an opportunity to explore some of the analysis tools available in the software. In the example above the 'gradient' tool can be used to measure the maximum rate for traces A and B. However, more importantly, this approach

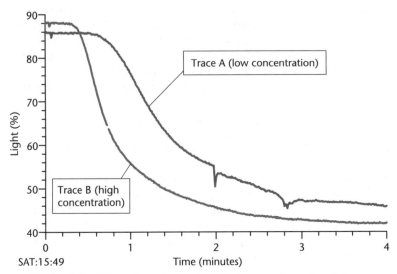

Figure 3.3   Effect of concentration on the rate of reaction between
sodium thiosulphate and hydrochloric acid

facilitates a discussion that enables the teacher to establish a link
between the data and the scientific model based on the movement of
particles. For a fuller discussion of this approach see the case study in *The
Identification of Training Needs* booklet for secondary science (Teacher
Training Agency 1999).

Whole-class practical on a limited budget

For many science teachers, being able to conduct a whole-class practical
activity with all pupils using data loggers simultaneously in place of conventional practical work would be the ideal. However, even if the resources
are available, some of the options discussed above may be a more productive and less stressful way to start. Even for those who feel confident
enough to get all the class using data loggers at the same time, they may be
constrained by the number of computers available. One possible solution
is to use hand-held, or palmtop computers in place of desktop or laptop
computers. Currently it is possible to buy data-logging software specifically for palmtop computers, which makes the latest models, which come
with a colour screen, a sensible budget alternative. Perhaps the ideal for
applications in the science laboratory would be computers with a high-
quality touch-sensitive colour screen, a standard keyboard and a size
somewhere between the palmtop and the current laptop.

Conclusion

In this chapter I have discussed issues related to making use of data logging in the school laboratory, following on from the general discussion of teaching and learning issues in Chapter 2. The final chapter of this part of the book looks in more detail at the issues of planning, classroom management and assessment by outlining three case studies of the use of data-logging equipment.

References

Birrell, I. J. (1996a) *Insight into Chemistry Experiments*. Edinburgh: Data Harvest.
Birrell, I. J. (1996b) *Insight into Biology Experiments*. Edinburgh: Data Harvest.
Frost, R. (1998) *Data Logging in Practice*. Hatfield: Association for Science Education.
Teacher Training Agency (1999) *The Use of ICT in Subject Teaching. The Identification of Training Needs: Secondary Science*. London: TTA.
Watt, A. (1996) *Insight into Physics Experiments*. Edinburgh: Data Harvest.

4

PLANNING, TEACHING AND ASSESSMENT USING COMPUTER-AIDED PRACTICAL WORK

Roy Barton and Caroline Still

Introduction

Each of the three case studies outlined below is designed to illustrate aspects of the issues discussed in Chapters 2 and 3. The idea is to provide a specific context for a discussion of the impact of computer-aided practical work on the core activities of planning, teaching, classroom management and assessment. The case studies provide examples from Key Stage 3 (pupils aged 11–14 years) and Key Stage 4 (pupils aged 14–16 years) and are set in the context of investigative practical work, illustrative practical work and remote data logging. The intention is to provide an opportunity to explore some of the different ways in which data logging can be used to enhance teaching and learning. More importantly, the case studies aim to exemplify alternative approaches and the different demands these place on resources, classroom organization and teachers' and learners' roles in the laboratory. The following key questions are explored:

- How does the use of data logging affect the learning objectives for science lessons?
- How should teachers plan for the introduction of ICT into their practical work?

- What are the alternative ways of organizing computer-aided practical work?
- How can teachers make use of data logging with limited resources?
- How can conventional activities be integrated with computer-based work?
- How are teachers to deal with practical issues such as file storage and printing?
- In what ways does data logging change the teacher's role during practical activities?
- What assessment tasks should we set when using computers in this way and what success criteria should we identify?

Case study 1: Key Stage 3 science investigation: factors affecting the stopping distance of a moving object

Introduction

Since the introduction of the National Curriculum for science in England all science courses have been required to include investigations, where the pupils are expected to have control over the conduct of the activity. Since one of the prime arguments in favour of computer-aided practical work is the way in which it facilitates the rapid measurement of physical quantities and thus helps pupils to focus on analysis, it is likely to be particularly helpful in this context. There are specific references to the use of ICT in science investigations in the science National Curriculum in England (DfEE 1999: 28).

Prior learning experiences

In the National Curriculum for science in England there are four elements identified in relation to the development of pupils' investigative skills: planning, obtaining and presenting evidence, considering evidence and evaluating. While the overall intention is to equip pupils to conduct whole investigations for themselves, as part of their development, it is often useful to conduct partial investigations, focusing on some, rather than all, of the elements identified above. This case study focuses on a partial investigation in which pupils are asked to carry out an existing plan with the main focus on their ability to consider and evaluate the data.

Let us imagine that the pupils have carried out a number of investigations, but the teacher feels that more development is needed in specific areas. In this context it is helpful to be able to focus pupils' attention on specific areas of an investigation. The other main advantage in the use of partial investigations is that the elements presented to the pupils, in this case 'planning', enable the teacher to provide examples of what is expected from pupils.

The work is aimed at pupils in the last year of Key Stage 3, aged 13–14 years. We will provide a plan that focuses on the relationship between the initial speed of a moving object (in this case a toy car) and its stopping distance. The use of the computer enables the measurement of speed to be made as easily as the measurement of time or distance. The rationale for this approach is that the main focus should be on the exploration of the relationship between the variables involved and not on the measurement of the variables themselves. In this case there is the added advantage that the data-logging software enables pupils to type in the stopping distance, which is obtained manually, and then use the software to plot this against the speed measured by the data logger. Finally, the analysing tools available in the software provide the opportunity for more able pupils to conduct a more sophisticated analysis of the data. At a basic level pupils could use the on-screen cursors to read off from the graph values of stopping distances for a range of speeds, enabling them to establish that the stopping distance increases rapidly with increasing speed. A more sophisticated analysis would involve the pupils looking for a pattern in the data for stopping distance for increasing speed. If this was done, the software could be used to fit a curve to the data giving the coefficients for the power law relationship, in this case we would expect the curve to be of the form: stopping distance $\propto$ (speed)^2. Although this would be a challenge for the majority of Key Stage 3 pupils it is worth noting that an important benefit of using ICT is the ways in which it can provide additional challenges for the more able pupils.

It would be expected that prior to conducting this kind of investigation pupils would have been taught about the measurement of speed in the context of illustrative practical work. In particular, they should be aware of how a data logger can be used to calculate the speed of an object by measuring the time taken for a card, of known length and attached to the object, to pass through a light gate. When conducting investigations it is important that pupils have already been introduced to any scientific ideas and background information that are required in order to conduct the investigation successfully.

Planning issues

Since this a partial investigation it is easier to plan for the resources that will be required. For the purpose of this case study, assume that there are enough light gates, data loggers and computers for a whole-class activity. However, the usual problem of providing each group with enough space to run their moving objects (toy cars) is made more complicated with the need to arrange the computers. This requires some planning, but the use of extension leads can help the placing of computers in the most appropriate positions. An outline lesson plan giving an overview of the lesson is shown in Figure 4.1.

Topic: Investigating how the initial speed of an object affects its stopping distance		
Date:	Class: 9Y$_1$	Lesson length: 70 minutes

Learning objectives	*All pupils should:* (a) Collect sufficient data to explore the question. (b) Communicate in a scientific way what they have found out. (c) Know that stopping distance increases rapidly as the initial speed of the object increases. *Most pupils should:* (d) Repeat measurements as appropriate. (e) Use their graphs to point out patterns in their data. (f) Relate conclusions to their scientific knowledge. (g) Know that if the speed of an object is doubled the stopping distance is more than doubled. *Some pupils should:* (h) Identify a numerical relationship between stopping distance and initial speed (i.e. that doubling the initial speed increases the stopping distance four times). (i) Consider whether the evidence they have collected is sufficient for the conclusions they have drawn. (j) Make use of secondary sources of data (i.e. Highway Code) to compare with their findings. (k) Make practical suggestions about how the investigation could be improved.

Materials required	Per working group: computer (with Insight software installed), data logger, light gate, toy car with card, ruler. Explanatory sheet setting out the plan indicating the quantity they are to vary (speed) and the quantity they are to investigate (stopping distance), also indicating other factors which need to be kept constant. Copies of a pupils' version of the assessment requirements for investigations. Copies of the relevant sections of the Highway Code.
Safety considerations	Keep tracks separate to avoid pupils falling over moving objects.
Relationship to NC.	Sc1 statements: 2g, 2h, 2j, 2l, 2m, 2n, 2o, 2p Sc4 statements: 2d

Assessment opportunities

During the lesson	Discuss progress with pupils. View data on computer screens. Read written work being produced.
After the lesson	Mark the written report related to the success criteria identified (related to the learning objectives).

Time	Lesson outline
	Introduce the activity – explain what is meant by a partial investigation – in this case they will carry out a plan given to them and that their main focus should be on *considering and evaluating the evidence they have collected.* Reminders about the significance of this investigation to road safety – talk about reasons for speed limits. Present the plan to the pupils. Explain how this fits with the Sc1 requirements for planning. Identify how the plan illustrates what is expected from them when they set up whole investigations for themselves. Explanation backed up by a demonstration of how to use the light gate to measure speed (revision). How to measure the stopping distance. How to input

	stopping distance into the 'spreadsheet' in the software alongside the values of speed which have been measured.
20 minutes	Pupils conduct the investigation
40 minutes	About half way through the time for the investigation stop the pupils and via a question and answer session aim to re-focus the pupils on what is required in terms of considering and evaluating the evidence they have collected.
	• Are your measurements as accurate as you can make them? • Have you got a reasonable range of results? • Can you describe the results you are getting in a scientific way? • Is it possible to find a mathematical pattern in your results? • What is the best way to tell others about what you have found out? • Which part of the investigation is likely to give the largest error? • Do you have any ideas on how you could improve the investigation?
	At this stage demonstrate how extra data could be collected to explore 'gaps' in their graphs.
	During the rest of the activity encourage pupils to save their data periodically. Also try to avoid queues at the printer by getting pupils to stagger when they try to print out their data.
60 minutes	Stop pupils collecting data with about 10 minutes left of the lesson to enable time for saving and printing.
	Provide pupils with a number of prompt questions to help them to focus on considering and evaluating the evidence they have collected – use a modified version of the learning objectives (but not giving away the relationship) to identify the success criteria for the written report.
70 minutes	Encourage pupils to look at the stopping distances in the Highway Code and to compare these figures with the results of their investigation.

Figure 4.1   Case study 1 lesson plan

How the learning objectives have been affected by the use of ICT

Although the learning objectives are taken from the general requirements for scientific enquiry identified in the science National Curriculum for England, there are a number of ways in which ICT has had a crucial effect on the activity. The most obvious is that the investigation of speed and stopping distance in this way would not be feasible for a Key Stage 3 group without the use of light gates and the facility in the software to combine manually collected data and data collected by the computer. Indeed, this case study illustrates one way in which the use of the data-logging software enables novel activities not possible when using a conventional approach. Moreover, using the computer enables pupils to collect the amount and range of data they feel to be appropriate, which means the teacher can assess this general requirement effectively. In addition, pupils have the opportunity to see the partially complete graph while still being able to collect additional data. Having the graph plotted and collecting data to explore areas where more data are required is clearly good practice, but is seldom possible in practice due to time constraints.

The learning objectives related to science knowledge were modified as a result of using the computer. The accurate graph of the results enables pupils to draw conclusions not affected by their ability to construct a graph or to draw the best-fit line. The ability to read data values from the graph on the computer screen will provide more opportunity for pupils to explore the numeric relationship between the variables. There is even a possibility for the most able pupils to use the 'trial fit' facility in the software to explore the equation relating the two variables, as discussed earlier in this case study. Clearly this would be well beyond the ability of the majority of Key Stage 3 pupils but it would be interesting to explore in the longer term what impact these sorts of analysis tools will have on our expectations. I would contend that some of the limitations we associate with pupils' ability may be simply related to the lack of conventional 'tools' to support their thinking.

The role of the teacher during the activity

As in all investigations, the role of the teacher is a mixture of facilitating the collection of data and encouraging pupils to focus on the investigative task. It is expected that most of the discussions will be carried out while data are presented on the computer screen, which should assist the teacher by providing a focus for an exploration of pupils' ideas. During this time the teacher can demonstrate for pupils any relevant features in the software that will assist them in presenting information and, more importantly, in looking for patterns in the data. As discussed earlier, it is possible for pupils first to explore their data qualitatively, which at Key Stage 3 may be sufficient for many pupils, but there are also tools such as those giving the coefficients for best-fit lines. Because the graphs can be produced dynamically, as the data are collected, teachers are given an opportunity to explore with pupils the idea of a best-fit line, since this will adjust as new data is collected. This would seem to be a particularly effective way of discussing what is meant by best-fit, a concept that many pupils find difficult and that is not easily explored via manual plotting.

Ways in which assessment has been modified by the use of ICT

Clearly the use of the computer means that it is pointless to assess the quality of the graphs pupils print out. However, since data collection is so easy pupils will have been able to collect both the range and distribution of data they required and would have had every opportunity to repeat any measurements they wished. Since the data will be presented so clearly, it will be much more apparent to what extent the pupil has been able to analyse them appropriately. The other issue is in relation to differentiation: the software provides support for the least able to obtain an accurate graph, which means that they are in a position to analyse and evaluate their data. As with other skills, pupils need practice in analysing and evaluating, which this approach provides. However, I have been surprised by how effective 'less able' pupils are at these skills when given the support of clearly presented data. For the more able pupils, the software tools provide the opportunity to progress further by supporting a quantitative analysis, as discussed above. One of the disadvantages of many conventional investigations is that they either limit the highest level of outcome available or have an entry level that is too difficult for some pupils. Perhaps the most significant contribution of computer-aided practical work is the way in which it supports and encourages the least able while providing a challenge to the most able.

Case study 2: Key Stage 4 using a remote logging application: the effect of pollution on the abundance and distribution of aquatic invertebrates

Introduction

Fieldwork is an important and enjoyable element in any biology course. However, incomplete and laborious data collection in the field can sometimes detract from the whole experience. On returning to the classroom there may be insufficient data in some areas to support conclusions, or sometimes an overwhelming quantity of data in others that is difficult to manage. Using computer-aided practical work it is possible to overcome many of these difficulties and focus on the underlying biological principles.

Well-oxygenated freshwater supports a greater diversity of aquatic invertebrates than poorly oxygenated water. An increased level of organic matter or fertilizers stimulates the growth of microbes and the resulting increased respiration causes the water to become de-oxygenated. Some animals are more sensitive than others to low levels of oxygen, and are therefore not present when the water is polluted. The range of invertebrates that occur at a site can, in conjunction with a published biotic index, provide an indirect indication of pollution levels and thus oxygen saturation. However, using an oxygen probe it possible for pupils to measure oxygen levels in the water directly. The alternative titration method using the 'Winkler' procedure (McLusky 1971) is a complicated five-day process and not very feasible in a school setting. Use of a data logger that can collect data away from a computer enables pupils to investigate the relationship between species distribution and oxygen levels easily. If the data-logging software used has a 'snapshot' option pupils can collect oxygen levels at various distances from a pollution source or at a range of depths from the water surface.

The work is aimed at Key Stage 4 pupils, aged 14–16 years. The work focuses on the relationship between the distribution and relative abundance of aquatic invertebrate species and water oxygen levels. It enables pupils to explore the role of microbes and other organisms in the decomposition of organic materials and the impact of humans on the environment.

Prior learning experiences

In this case study, assume that the pupils would have studied respiration and, ideally, have an understanding of the decomposition process. They have been introduced to the principles of adaptation and competition and are aware of the problems of sewage and fertilizers as sources of eutrophication. This lesson would make an interesting revision exercise for a number of biology topics for pupils in this age group, while providing light relief from the classroom environment. In fact, a simplified version could be used if you have access to a freshwater pond. The oxygen probe could be placed in the detritus-rich mud at the bottom of the pond, in the open water and at the surface. These three areas could then be sampled for invertebrates.

Planning issues

Oxygen probes are fairly expensive and have a limited lifespan, and so need careful maintenance. For the purposes of this study we will assume that only two probes are available. Working in small groups it is possible for everyone to obtain data for oxygen, as it takes time to sample and identify the freshwater invertebrates. Figure 4.2 shows an outline plan as a means of giving an overview of the lesson.

As possible extension work (using temperature, light and pH sensors), pupils could investigate:

- the effect of water depth on water temperature, pH and light intensity;
- the effect of vegetation cover on water temperature, pH and light intensity;
- the effect of distance from pollution sources (e.g. a sewage outfall) on oxygen concentration;
- the effect of distance from pollution sources on species abundance and diversity;
- the levels of nitrate and phosphate in unpolluted and polluted water using nutrient testing kits.

How learning objectives have been affected by the use of ICT

By using the data-logging equipment the pupils can make a direct quantitative link between the abiotic and biotic environment. Previously, pupils would have to accept that if dragonfly larvae and mayfly larvae were

Topic: The effect of pollution on the abundance and distribution of aquatic invertebrates.		
Date:	Class: 11 X₁	Fieldwork: 2 hours Lesson length: 70 minutes
Learning objectives	*All pupils should:* (a) Collect sufficient data to explore the task. (b) Communicate in a scientific way what they have found out. (c) Repeat measurements as appropriate. (d) Know that oxygen affects the distribution and relative abundance of aquatic invertebrates in their habitats. (e) Know that some organisms are very sensitive to oxygen concentrations and act as pollution indicators. *Most pupils should:* (f) Know that polluted water contains less oxygen and therefore supports a different community of organisms compared to unpolluted water. (g) Be able to use their graphs to point out patterns in their data. (h) Be able to appreciate how data logging can provide quantitative data to support the traditionally used biotic index pollution indicator keys. (i) Draw conclusions from their data and relate it to their scientific knowledge. *Some pupils should:* (j) Know that some organisms are tolerant of low oxygen concentrations and some may use anaerobic respiration. (k) Be aware that the level of oxygen will increase as the distance from the source of pollutant is increased. (l) Consider whether the evidence they have collected is sufficient for the conclusions they have drawn. (m) Be able to compare a published biotic index with data collected in the field. (n) Be able to make practical suggestions about how the investigation could be improved.	
Materials required: in the field	Per class: 2 data loggers in a protective waterproof case/ plastic bag, 2 oxygen sensors, extension leads for each sensor. Per working group: Pupil instruction sheets (explaining which environmental factors are to be monitored, which areas of water are to be investigated and how and where to position the sensors) 6 white trays, 1 bucket, 6 drag nets, 6 aquatic invertebrate identification keys, first aid kit.	
In the classroom	Computer, data logger, worksheets with questions targeted to meet the learning objectives, copies of aquatic invertebrate keys including pollution indicator species keys.	
Safety considerations	Carry out a risk assessment of the site – choose stable bank edges. Weil's disease – cover open skin with waterproof plasters, wash hands after fieldwork.	
Relationship to NC.	Sc4 statements: KS4 5a, 5b, 5f	
Assessment opportunities		
During the fieldwork	Discussion with pupils. View data collected on data logger.	
After a follow up lesson	Mark the written tasks related to the criteria identified	

Time	Lesson outline
In the field 20 minutes	**Activities in the field**: Locate two areas of water, one polluted and one unpolluted. Introduce the activity. Reminders about safety issues. There are 4 activities. Divide the group into groups of 2 to 4. Each activity should take about 20 minutes.
20 minutes for each activity	1. Identify and estimate the abundance of the invertebrates in an unpolluted stream. 2. Identify and estimate the abundance of the invertebrates in a polluted stream. 3. Using the data logger and oxygen probe collect data in an unpolluted stream 10 cm and 50 cm below the surface and at the bottom (using the 'snapshot' option in the software). Answer questions on the worksheet. In each case leave the oxygen probe in position long enough for reading to 'settle'. 4. Using the data logger and oxygen probe collect data in a polluted stream 10 cm and 50 cm below the surface and at the bottom (using the 'snapshot' option in the software). Answer questions on the worksheet.
TOTAL = 100 min activity (allow for change over time between activities) approx. 2 hours	**Activities 1 & 2**: Collect a sample from the water using a drag net (sweeping the net from side to side slowly in a figure of eight, three times). Empty contents into white tray containing some water. Count and identify the invertebrates using the keys. Repeat three times to obtain mean data for each stream. Spend 20 minutes at each site. **Activities 3 & 4**: Introduce the activity. Identify the factors that need to be measured and explain why these are important. Explain the advantage of using remote logging in the field. Are your measurements as accurate as you can make them? Pupils collect data for oxygen 10 cm below water surface and 50 cm below the surface and at the bottom. This needs to be carried out away from the activities 1 & 2. Reminders about the significance of this investigation relating to man's effect on the environment.
	Follow-up session in the classroom Download data. Try to avoid queues at the printer by getting pupils to stagger when they try to print out their data. Pupils are then asked to relate the oxygen values recorded against the abundance and distribution of invertebrates at each site. **Questions** Have you got a reasonable range of results? Can you describe the results you are getting in a scientific way? Can you identify any errors? Do you have any ideas on how you could improve the data collection? How does the oxygen concentration vary with water depth? How does the abundance and distribution of each species differ in each stream and why? Provide pupils with a number of prompt questions to help them to focus on considering and evaluating the data they have collected. Some pupils could look at the Environment Agency pollution indicator key to see if the data they have collected help to provide further evidence of the level of pollution in waterways.

Figure 4.2 Case study 2 lesson plan

present in an area, the oxygen concentration, by inference, would be high and biological oxygen demand (BOD) would be low. Using the data logger they now have access to a direct measurement of oxygen concentration at each site.

In addition, when using the computer the pupils are less restricted in the amount of abiotic data they can collect in the field. This provides the opportunity to discuss data reliability. They can make sufficient measurements to reduce error and obtain more reliable evidence. They can then judge the accuracy of the mean measured value by looking at the variation in the numerous repeat measurements. This facilitates a useful discussion between the teacher and the pupils about which of the data are appropriate for the study.

Using remote logging, pupils will be able to store data from the field and download them later back in the classroom. If the logger has a simple display, pupils will be able to monitor the data they are collecting, helping them to identify at which points further data collection is required. However, if one is measuring the effect of sewage outfall on oxygen levels and invertebrate distribution, a laptop available in the field would be particularly useful. Pupils are then able to observe the development of the graph as data are collected, again informing their data gathering. This, of course, is excellent methodology, but in the past time constraints meant that we could rarely achieve this in practice. Now we have the opportunity to do so.

As a result of using the computer, the learning objectives for this exercise, particularly related to science knowledge, will clearly require some changes. The focus will be directed more to the underlying biological principles and processes following the analysis and evaluation of the data, rather than the time-consuming construction of tables and graphs. Combining the oxygen concentration data with published biotic index values via a spreadsheet will provide an interesting extension for able pupils, or A-level students.

The role of the teacher during the activity

During the fieldwork the teacher will need to coordinate the collection of the data, ensuring that each group has access to the oxygen probe during the activity. Most of the discussion is likely to take place back in the classroom with the data presented on the computer screen, or ideally by means of a data projector.

Ways in which the assessment has been modified by the use of ICT

The focus for assessment will be based on the analysis and evaluation of the data and the understanding of the associated biology rather than the quality of the data presentation and corresponding graphs. As an extension activity some pupils may wish to progress further and investigate quantitative relationships between variables. The relationship between aquatic invertebrate species distribution and oxygen levels was previously one of inference. Using an oxygen probe the pupils can make a direct quantitative link between species distribution and oxygen availability. This evidence makes the whole investigation more tangible, stimulates discussion, increases motivation and may subsequently extend the assessment potential generally. This activity could also be used to assess areas of Sc1, particularly considering and evaluating evidence.

Case study 3: Key Stage 4 using an illustrative practical activity: electrical characteristics

Introduction

An important element in physics courses for Key Stage 4 in England is the relationship between the current flowing through an electrical component and the potential difference across it. Often this is explored by asking pupils to plot electrical characteristic graphs for a range of components. Since this area of study usually involves the collection and processing of large amounts of data it is an appropriate topic for the use of computer-aided practical work. See Barton (1998) for more ideas on the use of current and voltage sensors.

Prior learning experiences

In this case study, imagine that the pupils have already spent several lessons working on the topic of electricity. They have been introduced to the definition of resistance as the ratio of potential difference to current and have done experiments where they have made measurements using ammeters and voltmeters and have used these data to calculate the resistance of the component under test.

Planning issues

Clearly, the first task is to identify the intended learning outcomes of the lesson: see the lesson plan in Figure 4.3. However, the approach taken to achieve these objectives will in this case be mainly influenced by the level of resources available. For the purpose of this case study imagine that the school has enough equipment for half the pupils in the class to use the data loggers at one time and that there is also the facility for the teacher to display the computer screen for the whole class to see. This scenario has been chosen because it is relatively easy to imaging how the lesson could be modified as either one built mainly around a demonstration or one involving a whole-class practical activity. The lesson outlined also illustrates conventional activities being integrated with computer-based work.

The lesson planning needs to focus on setting up two parallel activities for the pupils, one computer-based and the other a paper-based task. The

Topic: Electrical characteristics		
Date:	Class: 10B,	Lesson length: 70 minutes
Learning objectives	*All pupils should:* (a) Be able to calculate the resistance of a component given values of current and potential difference. (b) Know that for some components the resistance can be constant but for others it changes. *Most pupils should:* (c) Be able to recognize, and be able to sketch, the shape of a current against potential difference graph for a fixed resistor, a filament bulb and a diode. (d) Be able to qualitatively describe the shape of the I/V graph in terms of the resistance of the component. *Some pupils should:* (e) Be able to use data from the computer-generated graphs to provide quantitative comparisons between fixed resistors, a filament bulb and diodes.	
Materials required	Half a class set of computers, data loggers, current and voltage sensors Per working group: 2 resistors, 1 bulb, 1 diode, dry cells, potential divider, wires Demonstration: 1 data projector, several components concealed from the pupils labelled A, B, C, etc.	
Safety considerations	No specific safety considerations for this lesson.	
Relationship to NC.	Sc4 statements 1b, 1c, 1d	

Assessment opportunities

During the lesson	Paper-based exercise will provide feedback on objective (a) Computer activity – discussion / questions and written record will give feedback on objectives (b), (c), (d). Also target some pupils to explore qualitative relationship i.e. objective (e) Q/A session during demonstration – feedback on objectives (a) to (d)
After the lesson	Review of answers to the written tasks during the lesson and pupils' answers to the homework task. Identifying the concealed components with reasons should also provide an opportunity to provide evidence for all the learning objectives.

Time	Lesson outline
	Introduction and revision: main points are a revision of previous work on how to calculate resistance (R = V/I). Main point of this lesson: does the value of resistance change or stay the same and how do we find out? Question to try to answer during this lesson: Why does a light bulb usually 'blow' when we first switch it on?
5 minutes	Set-up and organize two parallel activities – set clear time limits for changeover – (after 20 minutes). Explain to whole group the paper-based activity – then half the group collects the worksheet and moves to designated part of the lab, and starts work.
10 minutes	Briefing for the computer group: loading the set-up file, connecting the circuit and adjusting the potential divider. Outline the task on the Activity sheet. Monitor progress – discuss data with computer-based groups.

35 minutes	Groups change over – brief the new computer group.
	Monitor progress – discuss data with computer-based groups.
55 minutes	Move to front for teacher demonstration.
	Plot the characteristic for a filament bulb – discuss what the shape of the graph tells us about its resistance. Ask for explanation as to why the trace for reducing pd. is different from that when increasing the pd. Return to the question about why a mains bulb tends to 'blow' when first switched on.
70 minutes	Finally plot the characteristics for a number of components concealed from the pupils – pupils to sketch each of the graphs into their books. Homework task is to identify each component and give reasons for their choice.

Figure 4.3 Case study 3 lesson plan

teacher will also need to plan for the demonstration and discussion session at the end of the lesson. Assume that the pupils have become familiar with using the sensors, data loggers and software in previous lessons. However, setting up the software for an *XY* plot, in this case current against potential difference, as opposed to plotting the variables against time (*YT* plot), is something that is best done prior to the lesson, one option being to create 'set-up' files. This is done by setting up the software for the particular sensors to be used and arranging the graph as required. Before any collection of data this set-up can be saved as a file, which can be by loaded by the pupils as they start their activity.

The teacher would need to give careful thought to the instructions given to pupils and to how the data are to be recorded. Since the main learning objectives relate to overall shapes of graphs it is sensible to ask pupils to sketch copies of the graphs on to pre-drawn axes on their worksheets, rather than get involved in queues to use printers, which are often in short supply.

How learning objectives have been affected by the use of ICT

This case study is an example of the ways in which the use of computers enables the main focus to be on discussion and the analysis of the data. In this example the focus is on the comparison between characteristic graphs for the three different components. Although this could have been done conventionally it would have been at the expense of the practical work element, since it would not be possible to produce the number of graphs required during one lesson. In other respects the learning objectives are similar to the conventional approach but are more likely to be achieved, since more of the lesson time is devoted to them. For example, the last part of the lesson, involving the teacher plotting several characteristics in a short period, was an opportunity to reinforce the learning objectives, in a way not possible using a conventional approach.

The role of the teacher during the activity

As indicated in Chapter 3, this 'half-and-half' lesson is particularly challenging for the teacher during the lesson, and much will rely on the quality of the preparation and the briefing given to pupils. The paper-based activity will ideally not need much teacher input during the lesson. When the teacher circulates around pupils working on the computers they are likely to have graphs on their screens, which will provide an ideal opportunity to explore their understanding. This means that during these discussions the learning objectives are likely to figure prominently. Teachers can draw on these graphs by asking questions such as:

- If this line was shallower what would that tell you about the resistor?
- This line is curving. What is happening to the resistance? Do you have any ideas why?
- What is the difference between these two resistors?
- Using the cursor we can find corresponding values of current and potential difference. How do you use these to calculate resistance?
- Can you measure the resistance at these three points on the graph?

The written work that we ask pupils to produce needs careful thought. The nature of the tasks means that pupils will be expected to make sketch graph predictions using axes already drawn for them, or to copy and label graphs from the screen. This method of working, in which pupils are involved in making predictions, annotating graphs and constructing written responses to questions *during* the practical activity, contrasts with the usual sequential approach involving data processing followed by analysis. These tasks will also form a useful record when it comes to assessing pupils' level of understanding after the lesson. The computer-based approach enables teachers to pose questions and to encourage pupils to express their ideas and understanding during the activity by drawing on the data on the screen. For pupils (and teachers) who are more used to practical work mainly involving the recording of data in a tabular form, this change of style will need some getting used to.

Summary demonstration and discussion

This part of the lesson will, as with a conventional approach, be an opportunity to review the extent to which the learning objectives have been achieved and to deal with major problems that have arisen during the lesson. However, we can exploit the speed of data collection and presentation by collecting new data, which can act as the focus for these discussions. For example, this could involve plotting the characteristic for a filament bulb, which can then be used to discuss changes of resistance. Plotting the graph for both decreasing and increasing potential difference enables the discussion to return to the questions posed at the start of the lesson related to why bulbs tend to 'blow' when first switched on. This will provide the opportunity to introduce the effect of temperature on resistance.

Finally, the homework task can relate to yet more data collected during this summary discussion. The teacher can quickly plot a number of characteristics for different examples of resistors, filament bulbs and diodes, which are concealed from the pupils. Pupils can then sketch the graphs obtained and these can form the basis for the homework task, which involves pupils identifying each component from its characteristic graph and explaining the differences in terms of resistance.

Ways in which assessment has been modified by the use of ICT

Assessment of pupils' work when using the conventional approach would normally have been centred on the collection and processing of data, since that would have occupied most of the lesson time. However, the largely qualitative approach, involving a large number of sketch graphs, will not only have given the pupils a much wider range of characteristics to explore but will have been much more related to the curriculum requirements, in terms of overall shapes of electrical characteristic graphs. The sketch graphs used as the basis for the homework task are a quick but effective way of checking on pupils' understanding of a number of the lesson's learning objectives.

Conclusion

Each of the three case studies described above has illustrated some of the ways in which ICT can enhance science education. Although it is not possible to describe all possible modes of use, they have served to indicate how ICT can be used for pupils of different ages, and for work inside and outside the classroom and using different numbers of data loggers. In each case the lessons relate directly to realistic and achievable mainstream secondary science content but in ways that cannot be achieved by conventional means. Chapter 2 made a case for the 'value added' in using computer-aided practical work. This chapter has indicated how these ideas can be translated into action in the science laboratory.

References

AIDGAP (1995) *Key to Invertebrates of Ponds and Streams*. Shrewsbury: Field Studies Council.

Barton, R. (1998) *Probing Science: Voltage and Current Experiments*. Edinburgh: Data Harvest.

Clegg, J. (1980) *The Observer's Book of Pond Life*, 3rd edn. London: Warne.

DfEE (1999) *Science: The National Curriculum for England*. London: HMSO.

Hewitt, G. (1991) River quality investigations. Part 1: some diversity and biotic indices, *Journal of Biological Education*, 25: 44–52.

McLusky, D. S. (1971) *Ecology of Estuaries*. Oxford: Heinemann.

Part III

Using Information

5

USING THE INTERNET IN SCHOOL SCIENCE

Patrick Fullick

Introduction

This chapter examines some of the possibilities for using the Internet in science education: the use of the Internet in the classroom by students and by teachers; its use by teachers who wish to draw on Internet-based resources to produce their own teaching materials; and the use of Internet resources by teachers wishing to extend their own knowledge of science as part of their continuing professional development. I also explore how to find appropriate material, and the ways in which the Internet can be used for publishing and communicating information in science. Before doing so, however, I first ask the question: 'Why use the Internet in teaching science?'

Amidst all the hype of e-commerce, e-government and e-learning it is easy to lose sight of the real nature of the Internet as a communication medium. The railway boom of the mid-nineteenth century brought about far-reaching changes as a result of the ability to send goods and people over distances at a speed that had never before been possible. Exactly paralleling the rise of the railway network, 150 years later the opportunity to share ideas across the world using the global computer network called the Internet revolutionized the practice of science, enabling researchers to

find out about others' work long before reaching the stage of formal publication (see the physics e-print archives at http://lanl.arxiv.org for further
information about the archives and how they work). Continuing the process of change, in the early years of the twenty-first century we can begin
to see the Internet effect huge changes in science education as teachers,
students and scientists are put in touch to produce a global community
dedicated to the pursuit of science education.

As this chapter shows, the range of uses that the Internet finds in the
service of science education is vast – not just ideas about science, but ideas
about teaching science, methods of working, new computer programs and
simulations and much more can be accessed at the touch of a mouse button. Bringing classrooms, laboratories and homes closer together, the
Internet as a tool for science teaching cannot be ignored – it must be
embraced.

Modes of use by science teachers and their students

Internet resources may be used in a variety of ways by teachers and students. These can be summarized as:

- drawing on web-based material to be used by students both within and
  outside lesson time;
- teachers modifying and adapting web-based resources for use with their
  students;
- teachers using the Internet to support their professional needs.

Use by students

Many teachers report that, if students are to use the Internet 'live' during
lesson time, it is not sensible to ask them to search for their own material.
This not only deflects students from the activity but also gives the teacher
no control over the suitability of the sites located. It is much more effective if the teacher provides a list of suitable sites (with URLs) for students to
use, vetted before the lesson for their suitability in terms of content and
language level. At its simplest, such a list may simply consist of a series of
URLs provided for students on a whiteboard at the front of the class.
However, URLs are notoriously easy to mistype, and so the use of 'book-
marks' within the web browser itself is to be encouraged (see Figure 5.1).
Some teachers have created web pages containing links for students – in
this way, students can be provided with a single, simple URL that then
provides a list of 'one click' links to sites that the teacher wishes them to
visit. Since web pages are easily updated, sites can be added, removed or
edited very easily from this list. A page of links may be created for a specific
lesson (this has the virtue of focusing students' attention on only those

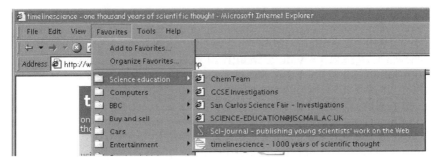

Figure 5.1   A bookmark for a site in Internet Explorer

sites of immediate interest) or as a page of 'useful sites' as part of a more general set of resources (see, for example, www.ringwoodbiology.co.uk/default.htm). As well as websites, there are a number of examples of printed materials that provide not only links but also suggested approaches to using the Internet in this way (Davis *et al.* 2000; Sang 2000). One point of which to be aware in using Internet resources is the speed at which Internet sites change and develop; a careful check of the resources that you are going to use with a class is always needed, preferably not more than about 24 hours or so beforehand.

To illustrate this approach we can consider using the Internet to support students' work on learning about the Solar System. There are a number of sites providing stunning images and detailed information on planets and moons (for example, www.solarviews.com and www.nineplanets.org). Students could be asked to use the text and images to compile a report on a particular planet, for example, using a graphical presentation package like PowerPoint, which they could subsequently use to make a presentation to the rest of the class (see www.webschool.org.uk/science/powerpoint/ for examples of a graphical presentation package used in this way, and www.educationusingpowerpoint.org.uk as a source of presentations for teachers and students). However, such an exercise needs careful planning, so that the students are directed to appropriate and relevant material and are not distracted by the wealth of other information available. To ensure this, the teacher needs to give the students a specific task, clearly indicating what is expected. For example, writing frames or tables to be completed could be used to help the students to focus on the most relevant information. Other examples of this approach include exploring atmospheric pollution, with access to local data and up-to-date large-scale statistics. One source of such statistics in the UK is through local authorities. Dorset County Council's Local Information Online at www.dorset-cc.gov.uk is an excellent example of this. (To find environmental information at this site, click on 'Environment and Transport', then 'Facts and Figures', then 'Environmental Data'.) Websites on smoking provide topical, and in many cases engagingly presented, data that students can draw on to explore a range of aspects of smoking and health. For example, the factsheets available from the Action on Smoking and Health site (www.ash.org.uk) provide a wealth of accessible information at a level appropriate for school use. Since students have increasing access to the Internet both in school and at home, research-based activities like these need not be confined to lesson time (of course, teachers must be sure that suitable access is available at school for any student who does not have access to the Internet at home before setting Internet-based activities as homework). Given appropriate structuring of tasks, web-based research, leading to the production of presentations using ICT, is likely to be seen by many students as motivating and fun, and can be used by teachers as part of a repertoire of activities designed to engage students and to enhance learning. Ofsted inspectors have noted that appropriate use of graphical presentation software provides students with many opportunities for group work, which can 'be effective as a stimulus for further research as well as supporting the development of [students'] planning skills' (Ofsted 2002).

An increasing source of support for science teachers is through sites funded by industry, which contain free resources for schools and other users. This follows a long tradition of industry involvement in science education in the UK, principally through printed materials. One such site, devoted to the explanation of nuclear power, is British Nuclear Fuel's site at www.bnfl.co.uk. Education resources are freely available here by clicking on the 'Education' link. Other examples include the timelinescience website (www.timelinescience.org), a project funded by a major pharmaceutical company, and schoolscience.co.uk (www.schoolscience.co.uk), a 'one stop' website containing resources from a variety of industries.

In addition to free resources, publishers and other commercial organizations are now beginning to offer paid-for access to resources over the Internet, often on a subscription basis. Such resources are usually advertised in a similar way to paper-based materials, in the *Times Educational Supplement* and by mailshots to schools.

Use by science teachers

The process of collecting and presenting information with graphical presentation packages like PowerPoint can also be used to good effect by teachers. An excellent example of such use is for teachers to model for their students the process of data collection and presentation described above. In this way, a teacher can introduce a task of gathering and presenting data about planets in the Solar System by carrying out this process in order to produce a presentation on the Earth.

Teachers can also look for ready-made resources on the Internet. In general these are often disappointing, since they rarely include stimulating material and often do not relate to specific curriculum requirements. An alternative is to make use of sites that collect together resources in a managed way. An example is provided by Research Machines (www. learningalive.co.uk). Part of this site is 'Living Library', which provides on-line access to a wide range of links grouped by subject and topic. Further advice on finding information about topics on the Internet is provided later in this chapter.

In addition to information in text and image form, the Internet has a number of resources that are particularly appropriate for science teaching. Applets, meaning 'small applications', are programs designed to run in a web page. These can be used to provide a simple simulation of an experiment or to help students to visualize an idea or process, particularly when a three-dimensional representation or an animation is helpful. A large number of good examples of science-based applets can be found on the ExploreScience.com website (www.explorescience.com). These are likely to be used for only a few minutes during a science lesson, much like a short video clip. The principle is illustrated in Figure 5.2. The position of the lens and the size of the object can be adjusted by dragging with the mouse and the focal length can be changed by sliding the pointer.

Clearly it would not be possible to use this applet as the principal method of teaching ray optics, but it is a useful interactive teaching aid (and it is free). In view of the ways in which teachers are likely to use these applets, it is helpful to make a local copy of the resource. One way of doing this is to make use of the option to make pages available offline when they are added as favourites in Internet Explorer (see Figure 5.3). Doing this means that the simulation may be run without connecting to the Internet – a useful strategy whenever access to a particular set of web-based resources in the classroom is required, in order to avoid problems due to access being unavailable because of connection difficulties.

On-line simulations are another useful resource to support science teaching. Geology Labs On-Line (www.sciencecourseware.com) provides a range of simulated earth and environmental sciences experiments that cannot be conducted in the school laboratory, including a 'Virtual Earthquake' program, which takes students through the science of an earthquake. This is an interactive activity with students required to respond to prompts; for example, by measuring data from the screen on the time between the arrival of the P and S waves. What makes this suite of programs so useful is that a certificate is generated when the simulation is successfully completed. This enables students to work through the program outside lesson time, and they can then provide evidence that they have completed the work by showing the teacher their certificate. This site also contains other simulations, such as radio-carbon dating.

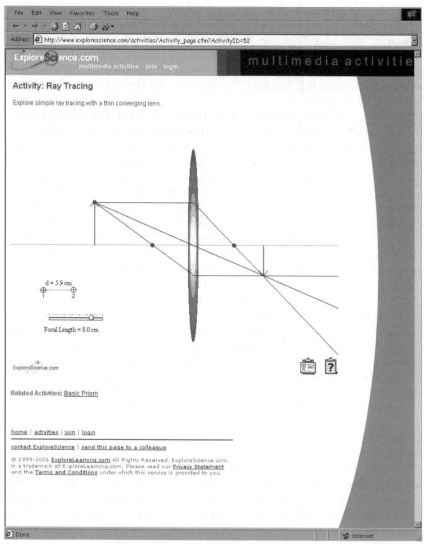

Figure 5.2 A ray tracing applet available from the ExploreScience website

The Internet as an information source for science teachers

The Internet provides an important source of information on examination specifications, government initiatives and inspection evidence. However, the specific needs of science teachers are catered for especially in relation to safety information. Organizations such as the Association for Science

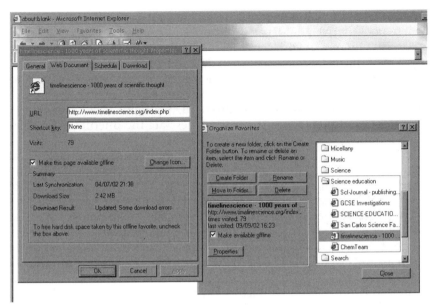

Figure 5.3   Adding a site as a favourite or bookmark provides the option of making the site available when the computer is not connected to the Internet

Education, CLEAPSS and SSERC (www.ase.org.uk, www.cleapss.org.uk and www.sserc.org.uk) provide up-to-date information and support on a wide range of issues related to practical science in school laboratories.

Using the Internet to find information

Locating information on the Internet if you do not have a specific address can be difficult. This is because the Internet is a vast library of information: 2.1 billion unique and openly available pages growing at a rate of 7 million pages a day in mid-2000, and set to grow even more quickly (Mark 2000). In addition, information on the Internet is highly distributed with little organization and is liable to change without notice (in respect of structure, content and location), and the criteria for publishing particular information using the Internet may not be clear to the user. Each of these presents the novice user with particular difficulties.

Finding information in a book-based library largely amounts to knowing where to look. Once a library user has an understanding of the library layout and can use the library catalogue in a rudimentary way, they are reasonably well equipped to find books on the subject that they are interested in with reasonable ease. However, the task facing the Internet user seeking information is much less straightforward, and has been likened to the search for an unknown book in a library in which the books are shelved in any order, and where books arrive and depart from the shelves in rapid succession (see www.asis.org/annual-96/ElectronicProceedings/palmquist.html for a discussion of the metaphors used when describing Internet use).

At a fairly early stage of the development of the Internet it became apparent that finding information quickly and easily would be a key issue in its use and development. To fill this need, two approaches have evolved, and these continue today. The first of these are the Internet directories, such as Yahoo! (www.yahoo.com).

Internet directories work by classifying information into a hierarchical structure. This structure allows the user to navigate through a directory 'tree' until the required information is found. For example, using Yahoo! to look for information about extraterrestrial life involves navigating from the top level of the directory (that is, the home page) to 'Science', then to 'Astronomy', and then to SETI (Search for Extraterrestrial Intelligence). Under this classification around 20 sites are listed in alphabetical order, from an ABC News report (Are We Alone?) to a site at the University of California.

Yahoo! is not the only directory on the Internet. Others include the Open Directory project (http://dmoz.org/) and Google (www.google.com). Directories specific to education exist too, such as Education World (www.educationworld.com), the NGfL (www.ngfl.gov.uk) and the UK Schools Resources Page (www.liv.ac.uk/schools/). These directories work by using people to find, evaluate and classify sources of information on the Internet:

> The Yahoo! Directory is organized by subject. Most sites in it are suggested to us by users. Sites are placed in categories by Yahoo! Surfers, who visit and evaluate your suggestions and decide where they best belong. We do this to ensure that Yahoo! is organized in the best possible way, making the directory easy to use, intuitive, helpful, and fair to everyone.
> (http://docs.yahoo.com/info/suggest/)

The type of directory being used will have a direct bearing on the kind of information being indexed, and the way it is indexed. This has direct implications for the search strategies employed; for example, a search using Yahoo! to find resources for teaching about global warming will find a wide range of information, of variable quality and suitability, while a search of the Virtual Teacher Centre in the UK (www.vtc.ngfl.gov.uk) will provide fewer links to sites, although these will be tightly focused to teaching the National Curriculum and GCSE, GNVQ, AS and A2 specifications in UK schools:

> Welcome to the Science area. From here you can access information and resources to support you as a Science teacher. Use the navigation bar on

the left to find information on ... links to web sites that have been approved as having useful curriculum content, as well as the Teacher Resource Exchange and other curriculum resources.

(http://vtc.ngfl.gov.uk)

The second approach to seeking information is to use a search engine. A search engine strictly consists of three components: the index, which is a searchable catalogue of documents; the spider or robot, which visits web pages and adds them to the index, indicating key works and other items on the page indexed; and the search engine itself, which is the software that searches the index in order to come up with a series of matches for an enquiry. Search engines in common use include Alta Vista (www.altavista.com), Google (www.google.com), Northern Light (www.northernlight.com) and HotBot (www.hotbot.com). Ways of searching for information vary slightly between search engines; for example, some require the use of Boolean operators like AND and OR, while others use check boxes and drop-down menus to hide Boolean searching behind a graphical interface (HotBot is an example of this). Ways in which documents are indexed by search engines vary too, which makes it possible that an unsuccessful search conducted using one search engine may prove fruitful when tried using another – see below. Many search engines offer the option to filter results in order to reduce the number of 'undesirable' results that are displayed (Alta Vista has a 'family filter', for example, while Google preferences can be set to 'safe search').

Advice on searching for science-related information

As discussed earlier, science teachers may wish to use the Internet as a source of information to inform their own teaching. The issue for the teacher here is to minimize the amount of time spent searching for information while maximizing the amount of useful material found. The ability to search for information in a profitable way is a skill that can only be acquired with practice. As a starting guide, teachers searching for information on the Internet should consider the following points:

- Is the information sought of a type that might reasonably be expected to appear in an encyclopaedia? If it is, then a visit to one of the online encyclopaedias like Britannica (www.britannica.com) is likely to be worthwhile, although full access to such sites increasingly requires a subscription. Even if a search within one of these encyclopaedias does not prove fruitful, the search is likely to turn up links to other sources of information on the Internet that may be useful.
- Is the information likely to be found somewhere specific? For example, images of space missions, information about space flight and data about

planets are available at the NASA website. Armed with a little knowledge about domain names, a teacher can navigate straight to www.nasa.gov without the need for any searching. Similarly, someone seeking information about the nutritional content of breakfast cereals in the UK might very well be better going straight to www.kelloggs.co.uk (NOT www.kelloggs.com, since this is the US site) than carrying out a search of the whole Internet.

If the direct approach to finding information does not work, then the next approach may be to try a directory. If a directory is available that covers the topic area being searched, this is likely to be a good starting point (for example, sites related to Key Stage 3 science are indexed at the ASE's site, and by the NGfL). Otherwise, a general directory like Yahoo! may be useful.

Alternatively, a search engine can be used at this stage. The choice of search engine is to some extent personal (and some schools or LEAs may recommend particular search engines that use filters to remove undesirable results), although the general rule may be regarded as 'more is better'. Points to consider when carrying out a search using search engines include:

- Use variants of spelling; for example, 'colour' and 'color'. Remember that many US spellings are subtly different from those in UK English, like 'specialty' (US) and 'speciality' (UK), 'aluminum' (US) and 'aluminium' (UK).
- Use variants of terms. Information about the nutritional content of 'biscuits' is relevant in a UK context, but 'cookies' may be more relevant if information from the USA is to be included too.
- Use more than one search engine ('A search that only uses a single Web search engine cannot be considered comprehensive or exhaustive. No amount of clever searching will unearth a record that does not exist in the database, and the databases of Web pages are all quite incomplete' (Notess 1998)).

Having found a source of information, there is a need to evaluate it. In a paper-based environment this may not be too difficult: we ask ourselves whether the book is by a reputable author, what his or her qualifications are for writing about the subject, whether the book has been published by a reputable publisher, when it was published and so on. Any or all of this information may be absent from information found on the Internet. It may be possible to make some judgements based on the URL of a site. For example, a site with a URL ending with .ac.uk is a UK university site, while one ending with .edu belongs to a US university. It might be possible to make judgements based on where the information is found, but since many universities allow their students and employees to put their own personal web pages on the university web server, this may not always be a reliable way of making a judgement. To assist in doing this, Robert Harris (1997) suggests the 'CARS checklist':

- Credibility. Trustworthy source, author's credentials, evidence of quality control, known or respected authority, organizational support. Goal: an authoritative source, a source that supplies some good evidence that allows you to trust it.
- Accuracy. Up to date, factual, detailed, exact, comprehensive, audience and purpose reflect intentions of completeness and accuracy. Goal: a source that is correct today (not yesterday), a source that gives the whole truth.
- Reasonableness. Fair, balanced, objective, reasoned, no conflict of interest, absence of fallacies or slanted tone. Goal: a source that engages the subject thoughtfully and reasonably, concerned with the truth.
- Support. Listed sources, contact information, available corroboration, claims supported, documentation supplied. Goal: a source that provides convincing evidence for the claims made, a source you can triangulate (find at least two other sources that support it).

What is true for teachers is true for students too. Asking students to use the Internet to search for information is likely to be a very hit and miss affair unless and until they have learnt to become sophisticated searchers. An Internet search is therefore likely to be a very inefficient use of time for students, and is probably something to be avoided unless either the students have learnt to use many of the strategies described above (including the evaluation of information) or the search is being used as part of the process of learning these strategies. For this reason, teachers should probably choose to restrict students' use of the Internet by providing links to pages that they themselves have already found. This is particularly true in primary classes, and in the early years of secondary school. Older students should be provided with greater freedom to search in order to provide them with the opportunities to become more sophisticated searchers, and to broaden their view of what is available to them in order to help them to become more discriminating about the type of information they find. Homework that involves finding information on the Internet may be problematic in that supervision is an unknown quantity where searches are conducted outside the school environment. This is an area that should form part of a whole-school acceptable use policy.

For students and teachers, a good introduction to the use of directories and search engines, together with suggestions for strategies for searching for information on the Internet, can be found at the Web Search Strategies page maintained by Debbie Flanagan at http://home.sprintmail.com/~debflanagan/main.html. The QUICK (QUality Information ChecKlist) site (www.quick.org.uk) provides a good guide to checking the likely quality of information, at a level suitable for 9 years and older. However, the tone and content make it likely that even considerably older children will still find the information appropriate.

For teachers, a detailed tutorial by Robert Harris (www.virtualsalt.com/

howlook.htm) contains information about evaluating Internet resources, and links to search engines, directories, encyclopaedias, periodicals and many others. Highly detailed information about search engines and how they work can be found at Search Engine Watch (www. searchengine-watch.com/).

Publishing on the Internet

Another advantage of the Internet is that work done by students can be published. Writing for an audience, other than the class teacher, is normally difficult, and students find it very motivating if they know that their material is available on the web, where it may be read by a potentially vast audience worldwide.

Publishing a student's work on the Internet is a much larger scale version of putting up work in a classroom display. A classroom display 'values' a student's work by putting it in front of a very limited audience, who may give some limited feedback. In contrast, displaying a student's work on the Internet places it in front of a much larger audience, and feedback may come from anywhere around the world if the work is associated with an e-mail address (which will of course have to conform to the school's acceptable use policy (AUP) on e-mail addresses for students) (BCS and NAACE 1999; BECTa 2001a,b). In the same way, many schools now regard their own websites as an important part of their image presented to the world, with students' work playing an important part. In addition to publication using web space controlled by students or staff at the school, publication of students' work may be done through involvement in on-line projects run by third parties. The nature of online projects can vary widely, and teachers need to be satisfied that the project meets the outcomes that they have set for getting students' work published. The Science Museum STEM Projects ('using the web to extend the educational potential of the National Museum of Science and Industry'; www.sciencemuseum.org.uk/education/stem/) is one example of an on-line science project that publishes work from school science students.

The ease of rapid publishing and communication provided by the Internet makes it an excellent medium for sharing and exchanging information. In the context of school science this makes it ideal for collaborative work between schools especially where science investigations are concerned. This is the purpose of the ScI-Journal project ('publishing young scientists' work on the Web'; www.ScI-Journal.org), a place where reports of school science investigations have been published since 1995 (see Figure 5.4). Taking work that students have produced during the course of their school science classes, the journal publishes each piece of work alongside a (moderated) discussion list. Visitors to the site are able to read the work and to comment on it by posting a message to the

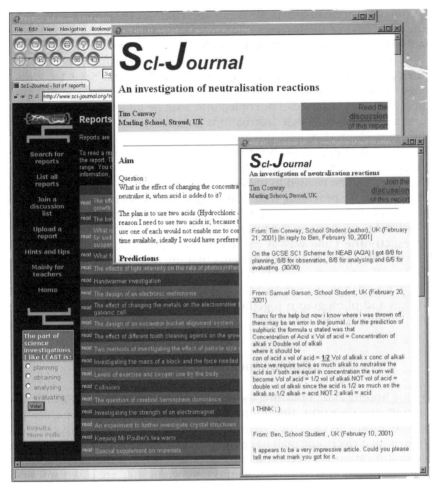

Figure 5.4   ScI-Journal contains a large number of reports of science investigations, as well as guidance on carrying out investigations and writing reports

discussion list. This provides feedback on the article for its author(s), and may lead to a discussion about the results reported, the methods used or some other aspect of the report.

In principle, publishing web pages on the Internet is very simple, but it can get very complex indeed. A web page consists of text and graphics (pictures) laid out on a page. The layout is controlled by something called html (hypertext markup language), which is the code understood by a web browser. Fortunately, simple web page writing requires no knowledge of html, although this knowledge does become important once more sophisticated web page construction is required.

The production of web pages is a far less complex business than it was in the early days of the Internet. Many recent word processing and desktop publishing packages can produce perfectly acceptable web pages from a document made up of a mixture of text and graphics simply by choosing the option 'html document' (or similar phrase) from the 'Save As . . .' dialogue box. If the document is saved into an empty folder, the files produced by the package can be copied into a single folder on the web server and all should work well. Instructions for getting the files from the computer on which they were produced to the web server depend on the way in which Internet access is set up from the local computer, and almost certainly a process called ftp ('file transfer protocol') will be involved. A password will be needed to upload files on to the web server – whoever is responsible for providing technical support for the web server will be able to provide the password, together with advice about uploading files.

School publishing on the Internet needs to conform to the school's AUP in exactly the same way as other Internet use. Of particular concern is information provided about students that might allow them to be identified by third parties outside the school, and that might therefore lead them into danger. General advice (see DfES 2002) suggests that the use of names and photographs together is to be avoided, as is the provision of e-mail addresses for children.

Communicating information

While finding and publishing information involves transmitting information in one direction, the Internet can also be used for communicating information – in fact, the origins of the Internet lie in just this purpose, from which electronic mail has grown. What follows here concentrates on communication between students, although science teachers may find e-mail discussion groups useful, especially when they are based around a common interest (for example, the discussion list set up for teachers involved in teaching the new Advancing Physics A level course; see http://advancingphysics.iop.org).

Sites like Mad Scientists (www.madsci.org, 'a collective cranium of scientists providing answers to your questions') make use of rapid communication around the world by connecting visitors to the website to scientists who provide answers to questions about science to which visitors have been unable to find answers elsewhere. This site contains a vast archive of answers by scientists to questions posed by children (and adults too), such as 'Why does it rain?' and 'Can a high energy electron–positron collision produce any baryons?' A comprehensive search tool enables users to look for an answer to 'their' question. If one is not found, the question can be submitted and will be answered by one of the many scientists on the panel to whom the questions are sent. Bearing in mind the number of questions submitted at sites like this, and that the individuals answering them are doing so in addition to their full-time employment, up to ten days should be allowed to receive an answer.

Communication between children and scientists has formed the basis of a number of projects in which practical investigations carried out by students has been guided by a professional scientist; the Student Researcher Initiative (www.shu.ac.uk/pri/) is a good example of this. Such collaboration usually involves face-to-face contact between those involved close to the start of the project so that all parties get to know one another quickly. After this, the use of e-mail enables students to maintain contact with 'their' scientist, who is able to provide support and guidance without the enormous expenditure of time and other resources that would be required to make physical visits to a school. As already discussed, direct e-mail contact between students and others outside the school is difficult to manage, and may lead to situations in which children are vulnerable. For this reason, e-mail contact of this kind may be restricted to a 'class' e-mail address of the type 'y8ab@schoolYname.hants.sch.uk', which can be easily monitored by the teacher responsible.

In some cases, discussion between students may be moderated using a web-based discussion list. This is the case with ScI-Journal (www. ScI-Journal.org), where each piece of work has a discussion list associated with it. Postings to each list are moderated before posting, and each contribution is accompanied by the contributor's name, status (school student, teacher, and so on), country and date. While this leads to a delay of up to 24 hours in posting comments to a discussion list, it ensures that there can be no contact between contributors to the list other than that provided by the list itself.

Interaction between students via video-conferencing is also possible using the Internet. With applications such as Microsoft's NetMeeting (which comes as part of the Windows operating system) children can see each other, send files to one another, 'chat' as they would in a chat room and draw on a shared 'whiteboard'. Full video-conferencing adds sound to this list, although high-quality communication in this way requires a broadband link to the Internet.

Direct interaction between students raises interesting questions about group dynamics, and about the possibilities for students at different cognitive stages to collaborate to produce cognitive gain. For example, one group of researchers have argued that interaction via computer-mediated discussion could help students to increase their understanding of the nature of scientific knowledge (Cavalli-Sforza *et al.* 1994) through mediated discussion of competing theories. Opportunities for interaction across boundaries such as Key Stage 2 and Key Stage 3, as found in many schools in the UK, may also be quite promising in this respect.

Conclusion

This chapter has provided an outline of the range of ways in which the Internet can be used to support science teaching. While there are clearly many new opportunities for using this vast resource to enrich science education, they must always be considered in a critical and questioning way, always asking to what extent they are genuinely improving the quality of students' learning. As with many other areas of science education, it is a matter not just of finding the teaching material but of selecting, from the very wide range available, those that are the most appropriate, and then using these resources in the most effective way possible. Inevitably, this comes back to the skill and experience of the science teacher involved.

References

BCS and NAACE (1999) *Promoting the Responsible Use of the Internet in Schools*. Available from www.naace.org/searchView.asp?menuItemId=2&resourceId=58 (accessed 22 October 2002).

BECTa (2001a) *Acceptable Use of the Internet in Schools*. Available from www.becta.org.uk/technology/infosheets/html/accuse.html (accessed 22 October 2002).

BECTa (2001b) *Information Sheet: Internet Safety*. Available from www.becta.org.uk/technology/infosheets/html/internetsafety.html (accessed 22 October 2002).

Cavalli-Sforza, V., Weiner, A. W. and Lesgold, A. M. (1994) Software support for students engaging in scientific activity and scientific controversy, *Science Education*, 78(6): 577–99.

Davis, H., Frost, R. and Hemsley, K. (2000) *Science Online: Practical Ideas for Using the World Wide Web*. Coventry: BECTa.

DfES (2002) *Superhighway Safety*. Available from http://safety.ngfl.gov.uk (accessed 22 October 2002).

Harris, R. (1997) *VirtualSalt: Evaluating Internet Research Sources*. Available from http://www.virtualsalt.com/evalu8it.htm (accessed 22 October 2002).

Mark, R. (2000) Study says Internet size to quickly double, *internetnews.com*. Available from http://dc.internet.com/news/article.php/411381 (accessed 22 October 2002).

Notess, G. R. (1998) On the net: more Internet search strategies, *ONLINE*. Available from http://www.onlinemag.net/OL1998/net9.html (accessed 22 October 2002).

Ofsted (2002) *Good Teaching, Effective Departments: Findings from a HMI Survey of Subject Teaching in Secondary Schools, 2000/01*. London: Ofsted.

Sang, D. (2000) *Science@www/getting started*. Hatfield: Association for Science Education.

6

MULTIMEDIA IN SCIENCE TEACHING

Jerry Wellington

Introduction

A wide range of multimedia is now available for science, covering a significant part of the curriculum. Multimedia can offer 'added value' to science teaching by virtue of its ability to animate, to include sound effects and speech, to use short video clips and to allow 'interactivity'. It can also be used to simulate real processes and allow learners to carry out 'virtual experiments'.

But there are caveats to consider in the use of multimedia. The first of these concerns portrayals of science. What images is multimedia presenting of science – as clean and nice, or problematic and messy? Do they give misleading impressions of science and what scientists do? Do they breed any misconceptions about scientific ideas, or about the nature of science? The second danger concerns whether the use of multimedia in science teaching is displacing important labour such as hands-on experimenting and investigating.

The chapter begins with some introductory remarks about science and science teaching and then goes on to look at what ICT is good at in relation to them. I then present a range of examples of multimedia. These examples happen to be 'on' CD-ROM but the same general issues would apply if they had been on the large 'laservision' discs of the past, DVDs, the Internet or any other platform. The chapter then examines 'the added value' of using multimedia in science education and contrasts this with the 'dangers' and drawbacks of multimedia use. Guidelines are also given on choosing and using multimedia in the classroom, with a suggested checklist for judging its merits.

Why use multimedia in science teaching?

What is special about science and science teaching?

Science, and especially school science, is often a very practical subject. It involves *doing things*, which is often one of its attractions to learners. It involves observing, measuring, communicating and discussing, trying things out, investigating, handling things, watching and monitoring, recording results. These are all things we see happening in the science classroom. ICT can help in virtually all of these activities, as other chapters have shown.

As much as science is a practical discipline, it is equally a theoretical subject. It involves, and always has done, thinking, inferring, having good ideas and hunches, hypothesizing, theorizing, simulating and modelling. Thinking and thought experiments are as important as hands-on activity. Science involves abstractions, difficult ideas and theoretical entities that cannot be seen or handled. Multimedia and ICT generally can help as much in this 'thinking' aspect of science as they can in the practical aspect.

Authentic and inauthentic labour

Modern ICT systems (hardware and software) are very good at: collecting and storing large amounts of data; performing complex calculations on stored data rapidly; processing large amounts of data and displaying them in a variety of formats; and helping to present and communicate information in an attractive, visual way, using different media, such as sound, video.

These capabilities all have direct relevance to the process of education, and they help us to address the key question of when to use ICT and, equally importantly, when *not to*. But a key issue for education is: when does the use of a *computer* in saving labour or in providing a learning experience take away another important educational experience for the *learner*? An analogous issue occurs in the use of computers and electronic calculators to perform complex calculations rapidly. This may be desirable in some learning situations, for example if the performance of a tedious calculation by human means actually impedes or 'clutters up' a learning process. But it can also be argued that the ability to perform complex calculations rapidly should be one of the *aims* of education, not something to be replaced by it.

The distinction between what counts as *authentic* (that is, desirable and purposeful) and *inauthentic* (that is, unnecessary and irrelevant) labour in the learning process is a central one for the use of ICT in education (see Scaife and Wellington 1993 for a fuller discussion). The notions of 'inauthentic' and 'authentic' labour should be remembered when we look at the added value of multimedia in the examples that follow.

Examples of multimedia for science

The science curriculum is fairly generously provided for by multimedia producers (although they do seem do have devoted most of their energy to the Solar System, the periodic table and the human body). I use several examples of widely available multimedia, from different areas of science, in order to illustrate the general points and discussion that follow. The disks chosen have been selected as 'exemplar' disks, rather than exemplary, although some of them can certainly be of value in learning and teaching science.

Cell City (Anglia Multimedia)

Cell City is a CD-ROM that allows pupils at Key Stages 3 and 4 to learn about cells. It could also be used by teachers in 'demonstration mode'. The disk relies heavily on the analogy between cells and cities by explaining (using a spoken presentation accompanying a video) that both have communication systems, mechanisms for importing raw materials and removing waste, a control centre and so on. The disk has a slide show, a glossary, lots of still photos and video with voice-overs and some animation. One of its main features is a kind of virtual microscope, which allows pupils (and teachers) to view various small objects (such as spirogyra, bacteria, the eyes of a housefly) at different levels of magnification. Some views are labelled. The CD-ROM enables pupils to see exactly what they should see when they look through a microscope. The software can be used to complement conventional microscope work and assist what can be achieved by using diagrams and verbal descriptions.

Seashore Life (Anglia Multimedia)

Seashore Life allows learners and teachers to take a 'virtual walk' on the beach and explore the animals and plants they find there. A number of interesting video clips (24 in total) can be viewed, over and over again if required, for example a barnacle feeding, seals swimming, a crab eating, a hermit crab moving house. There are also 13 animations, such as of a burrowing cockle. Each video clip and animation has text on the screen next to it to explain in words what is happening.

The disk contains a database of seashore animals and plants that can be investigated; another section, the 'Filing Cabinet', shows learners how and why animals are classified into different groups. All the disk's facilities can be accessed through a room inside a lighthouse full of familiar objects, for example clicking on the television leads to the video clips.

'All very well', the sceptic might say of the video material, 'but you can do this with a simple video recorder and a video tape.' Yes, but the point with multimedia is that it is *individualized*. Learners can view it in their own time, at their own pace. They can watch it over and over again, slowly, quickly or one frame at a time. The watching, and learning, process is tailored to and decided by the user. The disk also has the added value of direct access to the small piece of video required.

Multimedia Motion (Cambridge Science Media)

This disk allows users to look at, and analyse in detail, all sorts of situations involving moving objects, for example car crashes, golf balls, people running, a falling chimney.

At an introductory level, students can simply *observe* a range of interesting examples of motion without studying it quantitatively. For example, they can observe a range of car crashes, over and over again, to show the importance of 'crumpling' or to observe the effects of sudden changes in a car's momentum on the dummy inside it. In this way they can develop a 'feel' for some of the abstract concepts of science such as momentum, deceleration, and inertia. Other examples include:

• The weightlifter. Students can watch him doing a 'clean and jerk' and observe the way he uses upward and downward motion.
• Running woman. Students can play the movie and observe her motion frame by frame. Notice how far her feet are from the ground when they both *leave* it.
• Jogging woman. Again, students can watch the brief movie, then take it frame by frame. What differences are there between jogging and running?
• Lunar hammer and feather. Students can observe the hammer and feather falling, and be asked: 'How easily could you replicate this in the lab?'
• Train crash. Students can look at the crash between the train and the nuclear flask and listen to the audio sequence.

In total, Motion focuses on more than fifty video sequences of moving objects that involve forces: cars colliding; golf, tennis balls and footballs being struck; spinning objects; gymnasts and weight lifters; rockets and astronauts. These all present attractive, sporty images (incidentally, with a male football player and female tennis player). The moving sequences can be studied again and again just for the enjoyment of seeing the stresses and strains involved. Each sequence can be studied in slow motion, backwards or forwards, all at once or frame by frame. Younger students enjoy clips in Motion such as the falling chimney, or the ball being compressed just as it is struck. The disk is valuable just to introduce them to forces and their effects. As one student put it to me: 'It's not really practical to do it [experiments with moving objects] in school . . . you can't slow it down. You wouldn't be able to see it [the football] properly being squashed and you wouldn't be able to measure the velocity of the ball. It shows you things you couldn't see with just the eye' (Year 10 pupil; first quoted in Collins *et al.* 1997: 74).

The disk's unique feature is its analysis software, which allows older pupils to study the movement quantitatively. On each moving image, points can be marked using the mouse. Positions and their times can be tabulated and then processed, either to display a graph or to provide the data for calculations (see Figure 6.1). Thus velocities, accelerations, forces, kinetic energy and momentum can be worked out for cars, trains, balls, rockets; indeed, if it moves it can be worked on. Again, in the words of a pupil: 'You can put arrows on it and work out speeds and acceleration and stuff. You can't do things like that on a video – you've just got to watch it happen' (Year 10 pupil; from Collins *et al.* 1997: 75).

This is the innovative aspect of a disk of this nature, which helps to

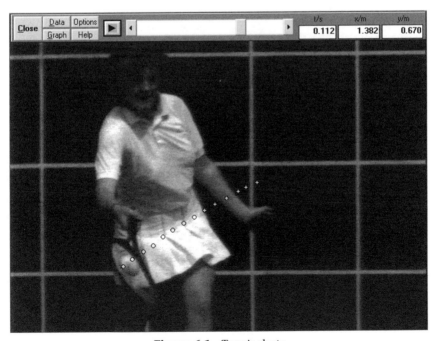

Figure 6.1   Tennis shots

move CD-ROM use in science forward from the passive entertainment mode to *interactivity* and truly provides 'added value' over traditional school practical work. One teacher commented: 'It's far easier, and safer, to do this on screen and take measurements, than doing it in a lab. It also plots graphs which can take some pupils an age to do . . . and it's easier for class control than running trolleys down wooden ramps.'

Forces and Effects (BTL)

Forces and Effects contains scope for plenty of interactivity with its Virtual Laboratory of experiments. Some are potentially dangerous and so are best done from the safety of a mouse and keyboard. Others could be done in the lab, but the value of having them on disk is that they can be tried and repeated over and over again, changing the variables involved indefinitely. For example, springs can be stretched, toy cars can be accelerated and decelerated, and many other situations involving forces can be studied on the screen. Figure 6.2 shows one example.

Again, pupils have expressed to me their appreciation of doing experiments this way: 'You can change things quicker and easier . . . it's more accurate doing it on the screen.' 'It's easier . . . and you can do a wider range of stuff, like changing the mass of the car and its speed, or its brakes and things; and you don't have to draw your own graph . . . it's instant and

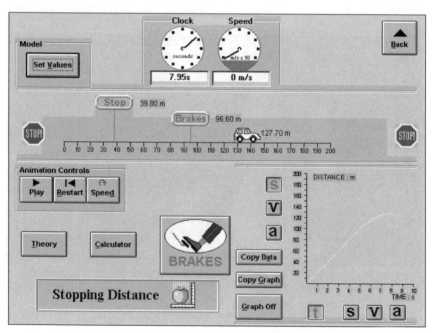

Figure 6.2 Forces and effects

they're more accurate; the graphs show things clearly' (Year 10 pupils; quoted in Collins *et al.* 1997: 76).

The Chemistry Set (New Media)

This is one of the most widely used disks in secondary science. The Chemistry Set contains several surrogate experiments and demonstrations such as dropping caesium into water (see Figure 6.3) and combining hydrogen with flourine – both of which are dramatic but dangerous to perform in the laboratory. How can this help pupils? 'It would help you writing up experiments . . . instead of just being told the order [of reactivity of metals]. You can see it for yourself so it stays in your head better' (Year 10 pupil). 'With the CD-ROM you get to see the good ones when the glass breaks [caesium in water] and good sound effects, you can hear them clearer. You can't do a replay in the lab . . . here you can slow it down step-by-step and catch everything' (Year 10 pupil).

Even experiments that can be done for real in the lab are, in the view of one pupil at least, better done on the screen: 'You get to see it as it should

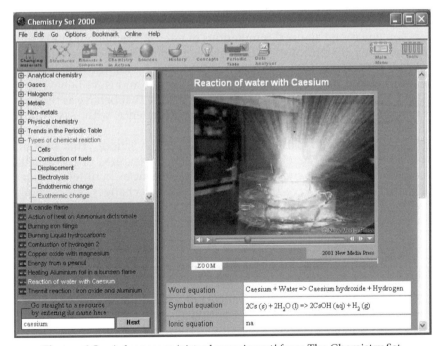

Figure 6.3 A dangerous 'virtual experiment' from The Chemistry Set. Image courtesy of New Media. Taken from Chemistry Set 2000. © New Media Press Ltd (www.new-media.co.uk, tel. 0870 444 1232, e-mail info@new-media.co.uk)

be . . . my teacher sometimes says: "That wasn't meant to happen". So he *tells* you what should happen. With the CD-ROM you're guaranteed to see what ought to happen' (Year 10 pupil). (As before, all comments were made to me and first reported in Collins *et al.* 1997: 72.)

The Chemistry Set is now one of the most widely used items of multimedia in schools in the UK (and elsewhere, such as Singapore). It contains a vast amount of material – representations, animations and experiments, many of which cannot be done in school labs, but many of which could. This is an issue discussed below.

Multimedia Science School (New Media)

It would be interesting to consider a larger number of specific examples of multimedia for science education. But the six considered here, this being the last, are sufficient to illustrate the general points and issues that I hope to bring out in the next section.

Multimedia Science School is a CD-ROM that covers several areas of science, from physics, chemistry and biology. For instance, one animation shows how the heart pumps blood. Another section of the disk shows photosynthesis with pond weed, which (unlike the real thing) works every time. The chemistry sections include a simulation of the Haber process, an 'equation balancer', simulations of rates of reaction and videos of many of the reactions of the halogens, which no sane teacher would perform in the lab due to the danger involved. In physics, the disk has sections on colour mixing, terminal velocity, half-life and wave behaviour – all of which allow 'virtual experiments' to be done that behave as they are 'supposed to' (in contrast to my personal experience with, say, ripple tanks).

States of Matter is part of Multimedia Science School. This uses an animated cartoon character to narrate the main features of the kinetic theory story. The disk enables learners to 'see' particles in different states of matter and to observe them during important changes, for example melting and boiling (see Figure 6.4). The disk certainly uses the power of multimedia to represent entities that students cannot see.

The added value of multimedia

Let us begin with the perceived benefits of using multimedia. In 1998, I carried out an in-depth study of multimedia being used in six schools. Each case study involved observing pupils, interacting with classes using multimedia to learn science, interviewing pupils in groups and interviewing individual science teachers. The full evaluation was published by the Nuffield Foundation. I also carried out an evaluation for the BBC of some of their multimedia material being used in secondary

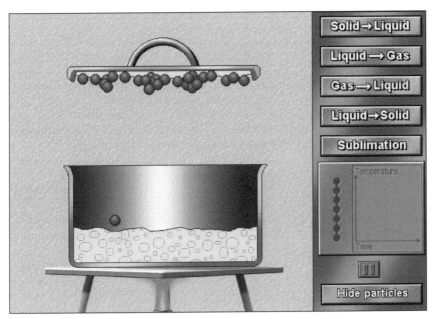

Figure 6.4 Simulation showing condensation.
Image courtesy of New Media. Taken from States of Matter Teaching Tool,
part of the Multimedia Science School 11–16 Edition package.
© New Media Press Ltd (www.new-media.co.uk, tel. 0870 444 1232,
e-mail info@new-media.co.uk)

schools – this involved collecting both teachers' and pupils' perspectives. The quotes below are taken from that evaluation (which has not been published).

First, teachers talked of the multimedia as being 'highly motivating and engaging'. They felt that it 'allows pupils to work at their own pace' and as a result can 'give pupils a sense of achievement'; multimedia 'allows differentiation by time, by route and by level'. The pupils' views were remarkably similar. They felt that it allows them to work as individuals, at their own pace, without fear of embarrassment: 'You can make a fool of yourself and no one will notice.' 'You can go over and over things.' 'If there was something you didn't understand you could go back over it, whereas in a lesson if you don't understand you don't say anything because you might look stupid or something.'

Many other points were made by teachers and pupils on the benefits of learning this way. For the sake of brevity, I have summarized in Table 6.1 the key points on the perceived value added to science teaching by multimedia use.

Table 6.1 Pupils' and teachers' perceptions of the added value of using multimedia in science teaching

1 Visualization	2 Differentiation	3 Motivation and variety
'Makes the invisible visible'	Gives enrichment and extension for able pupils	Generates enthusiasm, interest and involvement
Shows reactions not possible in school lab	Provides support and motivation for weaker pupils	Allows pupils to pursue their interests
Dynamic images and animation (unlike books) aid understanding	Allows independent learning, at an individual pace	Enjoyment, fun Visual impact, attractive
Images improve understanding of abstract concepts	Flexibility Allows easy repetition	Keeps attention or grabs attention
Enables visualization of processes too small, too fast, too slow or too dangerous to be seen in 'real life'	Allows more teacher–pupil interaction, better 'pupil contact'	Another 'teaching tool', a new way to present difficult ideas

The dangers of multimedia

Not the only way

So much for the perceived advantages of learning science with multimedia: there are clearly many benefits in the eyes of both parties (not least, incidentally, that pupils can and do use it to learn science at home; Wellington 2001). However, teachers and pupils in my evaluations were equally adamant that this should not be *the only way* by which science is learnt. For example, teachers were unanimous is stating that multimedia would never replace other teaching strategies. It would just be another valuable approach, which they could turn to when needed. Metaphors such as 'another string to my bow' or 'another weapon in the armoury' were common in teachers' comments. In reflecting on their own learning, pupils were just as capable of seeing that it would be wrong to attempt to learn all their science in this way. Some were even perceptive enough to state that multimedia is better suited to some topics in science, such as those that require help in visualization, than to others.

Out of the lab and into the multimedia system?

A number of CD-ROMs for science now allow quite detailed 'virtual experiments' to be done successfully and repeatedly on screen, without using up any of the consumables that science teachers can ill afford to buy.

This can be an attraction to some pupils, particularly those who detest traditional practical work: 'I like being able to do things over and over again, without anybody being able to see me . . . and it always works' (Year 10 pupil).

The key issue is whether this devalues scientific activity by removing some of the real, hands-on, authentic business of science and placing it in the realm of multimedia. For example, the Motion disk, the Chemistry Set and Forces and Effects contain experiments that are either impossible or unsafe for school labs and hence (in the view of some teachers) they more than earn their money. But should teachers be tempted to move practical science out of the messy world of the lab and into the virtual world of the multimedia system? What implications would this have for the future of school practical work and the way science is perceived by pupils?

Most teachers I have spoken to have remarked that fairly simple, traditional experiments, such as measuring the extension of a spring with weights on it, should be done 'for real': 'If my pupils used multimedia all the time they would never learn to use their hands and to do simple manipulative jobs like screwing a clamp to a stand or taking the top out of an acid bottle.' One pupil was clear about what should be done 'live' and what should be 'virtual': 'With a CD-ROM it's not like doing the experiment yourself, it's not live. If you can do them yourself, I think you should; but if a teacher has to do it, or you're just told about it, it ought to be on here [CD-ROM]' (both quoted in Collins *et al.* 1997: 75).

My own view is that, if relied on exclusively, the use of such CD-ROMs in science teaching would displace important labour, that is hands-on experimenting, investigating and the opportunity to develop manipulative skills. But if multimedia use is a *complement* to good practical work rather than a replacement for it, then its place in science can be justified and it will add value, not take it away. I leave the final word to a group of four Year 12 girls from a Leicestershire school who were reflecting on their GCSE science work and between them succeed in summing up the main issues:

Girl 1: If you did all your chemistry experiments on the actual screen . . . that would drive me mad.

Girl 2: Would it? I'd love it. I'd love to do it on screen so that you can see what's *supposed* to happen.

Girl 3: It would cost schools a lot less money . . . especially on things that break!

Girl 1: You wouldn't remember it as well as if you actually did the experiment.

Girl 2: But you could do it both ways . . . as a revision or a reminder.

Girl 4: Yes, when you're learning you need as many of your different senses as possible . . . like hearing with the voice-overs, and reading off the screen, and touch when you do it for real.

Girl 1: It helps if you've actually done it yourself. If you do something, then you do it on screen you know what it's for and what everything looks like. I definitely think if you've got 'hands-on' it helps you to remember it.

Misrepresentations of science concepts and science itself

Multimedia has the power not only to represent the 'invisible', but also to misrepresent abstract ideas. Equally, the images of scientific method and process portrayed by multimedia are a distortion of the complex and messy reality of science.

Breeding misconceptions?

Images have the power to mislead as well as to motivate or educate. Some of the more difficult and abstract concepts of science are increasingly being portrayed on screen by multimedia applications. The portrayal may involve an attractive and attention-grabbing animation. But can these images, often of abstract concepts, breed misconceptions? For example, in Electricity and Magnetism (BTL) electric current is shown in blue and red. The red current comes from the positive side of a battery, then becomes blue after 'travelling through' a bulb or other device. Current is thus depicted as a steady stream of particles shown by dots on the screen leaving a battery, changing colour and then returning back to the other pole of the battery (negative). Animations and analogies can be valuable in teaching difficult concepts. But the danger is that learners will see this as the 'correct representation' of electric current rather than an analogy to help understanding. A pupil once asked me: 'Does current change from red to blue after it goes through a light bulb?'

Messages about science

More generally, to what extent will the use of disks for this kind of 'virtual practical work' affect pupils' views of science and scientific activity? Do they present it as 'clean and unproblematic' when in reality it is a complex, highly problematic venture? Virtual experiments never 'go wrong'.

The old adage of school science practicals – 'if it moves it's biology, if it smells it's chemistry, if it doesn't work it's science' – becomes obsolete with multimedia. Living things do not inhabit CD-ROMs, smell is not yet an output of computer systems and virtual science experiments never go wrong. We have the experiments of science such as stretching springs, measuring speeds and connecting electric circuits working every time and repeatable at will. Students will need to find new jokes and insults to aim at the science teacher in the white coat (which, incidentally, becomes unnecessary).

This is obviously an overstatement of the practical shifts that could result from multimedia use in science. But analyses of media coverage (especially in the newspapers) of science show that it is portrayed as 'whizz-bang and dramatic; a disconnected rag-bag of work and discovery; certain; individual; and sudden, not based on earlier work' (Wellington 1991: 370; these points are expanded in that article). There is a danger that growing multimedia use in education will add to that portrayal. In reality scientific experiments are extremely difficult to repeat and replicate successfully and they do often go wrong; science usually proceeds slowly and carefully, by accretion; it is largely based on teamwork rather than individual 'crackpot' discoveries; and it is often a very inexact and unclean activity.

One of the stated requirements of the English National Curriculum is to teach pupils about the nature of science and scientific ideas. Exclusive use of multimedia to replace hands-on practical activity will produce a distorted view of the nature of science and fail to fulfil this statutory requirement. Virtual reality is clean and simple. Real life and real phenomena are messy and complex. Newton's laws, for example, do apply to real life (on Earth) but they are far easier to see or visualize in a virtual reality situation that can give us frictionless objects, point masses and objects that carry on moving for ever in a straight line in the absence of an external force. The neatness and simplicity of virtual reality is at one and the same time both its strength and its weakness. This is why learners of science (which is the study of the *natural* world) must experience both.

Choosing and using multimedia for the classroom

Reviewing and evaluating multimedia

One of the skills that is valuable to teachers is the ability to judge or evaluate items of software both before and after its use. If you don't like it or it won't 'work' in your department, don't buy it. Teachers also need to develop the ability and experience to look back on an application of ICT and evaluate its success.

Judging and evaluating software (just like assessing 'good' science textbooks) comes with intuition and experience but it can also be valuable to have a set of points or a checklist to aid your intuition. The points below (some obvious, others not so obvious) are designed as a framework to help in reviewing ICT, both before and after you use it. Most of them are not science specific.

- Does it fit the curriculum? Does it support your learning goals?
- Does it fit the learners? Is the depth of treatment right for the audience? Does it suit the ability range within a class?

- Does it fit the time slot? For example, does it suit a five-minute demonstration, pupils taking short turns or whole lesson use in a computer room?
- Does it fit the hardware? If the software is on CD-ROM, can it be used with a network of computers? Does it need demonstrating on a large screen?
- Does it enhance science education? Can it do things better than we can normally? Does it encourage problem solving, investigating, modelling, classifying, sorting, questioning, pattern finding, data exploring, researching, group work, out of class work?
- Does it fit the teachers? Is it easy to get started? Does the effort put in to use it produce a pay-off? Does the manual say how you're supposed to teach with it? Is it possible to customize the software to suit your approach?

The key question, of course, is: what added value does it offer in learning *and* teaching science?

Table 6.2 lists the questions I use in examining or reviewing multimedia for science education. I offer this as a possible checklist and would be pleased to hear from anyone who would like to add to it or comment on it.

Table 6.2 A possible checklist for evaluating multimedia

Are the language levels (spoken and written text) appropriate?

How well are animation, video and audio used in explanations?

Does the disk give any misleading impressions of science concepts, e.g. energy, electric current, force; or of science itself?

Will it interest, motivate or excite students?

How much structure and guidance is provided? Is the disk easy to use and find your way around? Do you get lost?

Does it use 'virtual practicals'? If so, is this justified? Could they be done with more educational value in a school lab?

What modes of use does the disk offer: a tutorial, revision aid, simulation, virtual practical, database, encyclopaedia? How valuable will these be in the classroom (e.g. as an 'electronic blackboard' or for small groups) or for self-study?

Managing multimedia use in a typical school

Where is multimedia best deployed: in the science lab, computer room, library? We can list several modes of use that are currently in operation, for better or for worse:

- mode A, as a tool for lecture or demonstration, for example using a screen or whiteboard and a projector;
- mode B, using a single PC with one small group, for example as part of a circus in the lab;

- mode C, with half a class using up to five PCs;
- mode D, with a whole class, using a suite of computers, for example in the computer room;
- mode E, independent use (for example at home, in the library, in the learning resource centre), perhaps prompted and motivated by seeing multimedia used in the classroom.

Which of these modes are best for which teaching or learning purposes in science? Table 6.3 summarizes the pros and cons of the two polarized approaches.

Teachers will need to weigh all these factors up when considering how best to fit multimedia and ICT work generally into their schemes of work and their lesson plans. Unless they do become built in to plans and schemes of work ('institutionalized'), my experience is that they are not generally used on a department-wide basis – they only occur in the lessons of the individual enthusiast or ICT zealot.

Table 6.3 Computers to the classroom versus classes to the computer room

For	Against
Classes to the computer room	
Dedicated room may lead to: - tighter security - easier maintenance - ease of supervision (e.g. technical help on hand) - careful monitoring (e.g. of temperature, dust, ventilation)	Room may be seen as the province, territory or annexe of certain departments Multimedia use seen as a 'special' activity Prior planning, timetabling and scheduling needed (rules out spontaneity) Reduces integration with other aspects of classroom practice or curriculum
Computers to the classroom	
More likely integration into classroom practice and curriculum Seen as just another 'learning tool' Not seen as the property of one department more than another Spontaneous, unplanned use made possible	Problems of: - security - adequate facilities - environmental conditions e.g. chalk dust, water, chemicals Technical support not on hand

Conclusion

My own view is that teachers need to look critically and carefully at the use of multimedia for science teaching, just as they would with any other item of educational technology. Like all other technology, from the knife to the motor car, it has the potential for both good and ill. Zealots who preach about the benefits of ICT and the 'power of the Internet' need to bear this simple platitude in mind (indeed, the Internet needs to be watched even more carefully than the CD-ROM simply because it propagates unpackaged, unfiltered and unchecked information; at least most CD-ROMs have been checked for accuracy, proofread and edited).

My suggestion is that the following 'health warning' questions should be asked by teachers who are critically examining multimedia applications for science education:

- What messages do its images convey about science as a discipline? Does it present a distorted view of science?
- What purposes do its images or animations serve? What added value do the sounds and images provide? On the other hand, what misconceptions might an image create?
- Do images replace text or supplement and complement it?
- Does the use of multimedia displace important, 'authentic' activity, such as first-hand experience, for learners?

On a more positive note, multimedia does have considerable advantages over other resources, such as a book or even a teacher. In summary, multimedia can offer the following:

1 Audio. A CD-ROM can provide speech and sound effects, which can sometimes help in teaching an idea or a concept; it can also attract and motivate learners.
2 Animation. Books can include diagrams but cannot provide the animation that a computer program or multimedia package can.
3 Video. Many CD-ROMs provide useful short video clips (although their quality is, as yet, commonly quite poor).
4 Interactivity and tutorial help. Books are non-interactive in that they cannot provide feedback on a learner's progress. Multimedia can be interactive, although this word is overused.
5 Substitutes for practical work. Multimedia can provide many possibilities for practical or 'field' work that other resources cannot; for example, virtual experiments, simulations, real-life situations to study, surrogate walks, demonstrations.

We need to recognize these attributes and possibilities, and examine each application to see what 'added value' it can provide. We also need to be wary of wild claims often made for the advantages of using multimedia in learning. The main criterion is that multimedia should be able to enrich science teaching and to motivate learners of science, that is to add to both the cognitive and the affective domains. Unless it does this, then why use it?

References

Collins, J., Hammond, M. and Wellington, J. J. (1997) *Teaching and Learning with Multimedia*. London: Routledge.
Scaife, J. and Wellington, J. J. (1993) *IT in Science and Technology Education*. Buckingham: Open University Press.
Turkle, S. (1984) *The Second Self: Computers and the Human Spirit*. London: Granada.
Underwood, J. and Underwood, G. (1990) *Computers and Learning*. Oxford: Basil Blackwell.
Weizenbaum, J. (1984) *Computer Power and Human Reason*. Harmondsworth: Penguin.
Wellington, J. J. (1985) *Children, Computers and the Curriculum*. London: Harper and Row.
Wellington, J. J. (1989) *Education for Employment: The Place of Information Technology*. Windsor: NFER-Nelson.
Wellington, J. J. (ed.) (1998) *Practical Work in Science: Which Way Now?* London: Routledge (various chapters including those by Baggott, Wardle and Barton).
Wellington, J. J. (1991) Newspaper science, school science: friends or enemies?, *International Journal of Science Education*, 13(4): 363–72.
Wellington, J. J. (2001) Exploring the secret garden: the growing importance of ICT in the home, *British Journal of Educational Technology*, 32(2): 233–44.

The full report of the evaluation mentioned in this chapter, entitled *Multimedia in Science Teaching*, is available free from Nuffield Curriculum Projects, 28 Bedford Square, London WC1B 3EG. It can also be accessed from the website http://www.chemistryschool.com. The BBC evaluation mentioned here has not been made public, except in the quotes above.

Part IV

Interpreting Data

7

HANDLING AND INTERPRETING DATA IN SCHOOL SCIENCE

John Wardle

What do pupils do in science lessons?

The purpose of the science curriculum is multiple and has been well documented by other authors (Milner 1986; Millar 1996). It is not just about absorption of information. There is something extra that provides a unique element to science education. This is in the way it deals with the exploration of the physical world, frequently but not exclusively through experimentation and the interpretation of data collected from such explorations. This latter process is the crucial aspect of this learning process, promoting the experiment to a higher level than just a physical experience. It is about seeing the world in a different way, not just from concrete observations or description. It is about looking at the results of investigations and making some connection with the real world. It is about having and using the skills and processes to enable this to happen. It is about developing and progressing these skills. It is about making sense of the data collected.

The pedagogic issues of developing knowledge and understanding are more complex than the simple acquisition of facts and are important issues to be considered by teachers. The processing of data and assimilation into knowledge and understanding can be supported in many ways by the use of ICT, particularly spreadsheets, databases, data logging and associated graphing tools, commonly referred to as data-handling tools. This chapter concentrates on the use of spreadsheets and related software, looking at how knowledge and understanding can be developed through data handling, and considers the implications for science teachers.

The 'process science' movement of the 1970s and 1980s raised awareness of the importance of teaching pupils how to 'do' science, often to the exclusion of scientific content. As with many trends in education, the pendulum has swung back in the UK to a content-led curriculum, largely brought about by the introduction of the National Curriculum. Importantly, elements of the process approach have been retained, forming the basis of Attainment Target 1, Scientific Enquiry, in the National Curriculum for England. Most science educators would agree that there needs to be a balance between the processes and content elements of the science curriculum.

In the National Curriculum for Science in England, the programme of study for Attainment Target 1 (Sc1 Scientific Enquiry) sets out the framework for the investigative process (DfEE and QCA 1999). Process skills can be found under the strands of this framework (planning, obtaining and presenting evidence, considering evidence and evaluating). Making predictions, controlling variables, presenting results, identifying and describing patterns and trends, drawing conclusions from data and considering anomalies have to be taught to, and used by, pupils studying the National Curriculum between the ages of 11 and 16. Good teaching will draw upon a range of strategies to help pupils to learn. ICT may be one apposite strategy to be called on in certain teaching situations.

Tools for data handling

The common tools for supporting data-handling tasks in school include spreadsheets, databases, graphing tools, calculators and software dedicated to specific tasks. Software developments have resulted in a convergence in functionality of these tools. This simplifies the selection of the tool for use in the classroom, and factors such as whether it is fit for purpose, user familiarity and availability are likely to be the major considerations, providing the tool meets the basic level of functionality.

There are standard procedures that pupils carry out during the course of their science lessons. For example, in a typical experiment, pupils will record their results in tabular format, calculate a value from the data (for example, the average), create a new column of data (such as the reciprocal of a data set) and graph the data. If they are working with a large data set then searching, filtering and sorting the data may be additional processes to be carried out.

The software must offer the following functionality:

- tabulate data in columns;
- carry out calculations;
- sort the data into order;
- search for specific values;
- generate new data sets;
- graph or chart the data;
- calculate.

It is unlikely that all these features will be used in every pupil task. The tools offer more functionality than is generally needed (the range of formulae in a spreadsheet far exceeds the demands of school science). There should be no difficulty in finding a software tool capable of fulfilling the needs of data-handling tasks in the classroom.

Many of these tools are referred to as 'generic' software. This means that they are available in a similar format with similar functionality from different software producers. For a teaching situation, independence of the task from the software is a positive advantage. Generic software is widely available, often pre-loaded on computers or provided as part of an integrated suite of programs. These factors make the use of generic software attractive in school in terms of both accessibility and cost (see Figure 7.1).

Generic software is adaptable to many different situations (a spreadsheet can be used for a range of tasks, from plotting extension against load to

This spreadsheet will help you to work out the cost of running different appliances in your home

you can change any information written in white or add to pale blue columns – the spreadsheet will calculate and show results in yellow

Cost per unit of electric = 6.19	Total cost per day = £ 0.65
number of days = 365	Total cost = £ 237.42

Name of appliance	Number of appliances	Power (W)	Power (kW)	Time (hrs)	Time (mins)	Units	Cost (p)
T.V.	3	150	0.45	4		1.80	11.14
kettle	10	2200	22		4	1.47	9.08
washing machine		2400	2.4	1		2.40	14.86
lights	8	100	0.8	5		4.00	24.76
computer		75	0.075	3		0.23	1.39
iron		1600	1.6		20	0.53	3.30
toaster		500	0.5		10	0.08	0.52

Figure 7.1 Energy spreadsheet

modelling predator–prey relationships). This adds to its value in terms of cost but means that the teacher is faced with a framework of tools with no specific science content. Sample templates and files are becoming a popular source of content for these programs but in the first instance the teacher may be faced with creating work and generating content themselves.

An alternative to the generic approach is software that is written for a specific task. The converse of the above arguments applies to the use of such software: being written with a specific content, it can only be used in limited situations applying to the particular content, so the functionality will be restricted to suit the needs of the task.

The advantages are that such a tool is designed with a specific task in mind and that content will be included in this package. The example shown (Figure 7.2) illustrates these points in the context of diet analysis. Pupils can analyse the nutritional content of their diet by selecting foods from a nutritional database. They are limited by the content of the database, which may be restricted in its range of foods (vegetarian, for example), but can construct their own diet by entering estimates of the quantities of foods eaten. The software displays a tabular display of each food entered in terms of energy, protein, carbohydrates and other categories, and a graphical summary of the overall diet related to recommended daily amounts. There is flexibility within the package but the pupil is con-

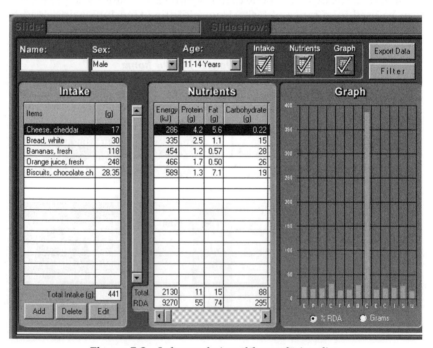

Figure 7.2   Software designed for analysing diets

strained to looking at diets. All calculations and outputs are controlled and processed within the software, eliminating the need to understand formulae or select type of graphs. This enables the pupil, in learning terms, effectively and economically to access the scientific information needed and make the interpretations and evaluations of the data presented, rather than being involved in the mechanical process of producing the information.

The choice of software to support any teaching activity needs to be firmly embedded in the planning cycle of the lesson. The objectives of the lesson define the content of the lesson. Strategies and activities selected by the teacher should enable these objectives to be met in the most effective way for the group of pupils involved. There will be teaching situations that lend themselves to an ICT led or supported approach and different software packages will be more or less applicable. The skill of the teacher lies within this decision-making process. Contrary to some popular opinion, this reinforces rather than replaces the role of the teacher when ICT is used in the classroom.

Table 7.1 Typical properties of data-handling software

	Calculate	Graph or chart	Organize in table	Sort	Search	Generic	Content
Spreadsheet	✔	✔	✔	✔	✔	✔	✘
Database	✔	✔	✘	✔	✔	✔	✘
Graphing tool	✘	✔	✔	✘	✘	✔	✘
Calculation	✔	✘	✘	✘	✘	✔	✘
Content-specific tool	✔	✔	✔	✔	✘	✘	✔

Recording and reporting results

In most science curricula there is great emphasis placed on the practical approach to learning science. To support pupils in recording and presenting evidence, either as part of a conventional illustrative practical activity or as part of a pupil-directed investigation, spreadsheets can be used. The software can act as a programmable calculator to support pupils as they process their data or as a graphing tool to support the presentation of the data. Whatever the use, the teacher should assess the learning gains. This might use criteria such as effectiveness, added value to the science learning and development of study skills. Scaife and Wellington (1993) refer to additional advantages of using spreadsheets, such as flexible learning, group work, improved teacher confidence and competence, which are perhaps less tangible benefits but equally valuable gains.

Scenario 1

There are a series of experiments that require pupils to make measurements and work out a result, often using a formula, from these measurements. The science objectives in this type of activity should relate to developing pupils' understanding of the topic being covered. A typical example might be in finding out how much energy there is stored in foods.

The standard class practical for this topic involves burning a peanut (though with increasing concern over nut allergies, imaginative alternatives ranging from dried fruits to pasta are appearing in the school laboratory) under a test tube of water and measuring the temperature rise in the water. The practical would be organized as a class experiment and carried out in small groups.

To find out the energy locked in the peanut (or other food) a calculation is done using the specific heat capacity (shc) of the water, rise in temperature and mass of water (energy = mass × temp. rise × shc). This experiment is frequently carried out with pupils aged between 12 and 14 and at this level pupils are unlikely to have an understanding of the concept of specific heat capacity. Their use of the formula is a means to an end in order to find and appreciate the energy value of the peanut and to understand the concept that the food contains 'stored' energy. Using technology to support pupils in this situation is therefore a valid strategy. If the objective were to teach them the formula for calculating energy content, using the spreadsheet would not be such a suitable strategy.

Before the lesson, the teacher prepares a spreadsheet for recording the results of the experiment, in the form of a template. This will act as a calculating aid for the pupils. The formula for working out the energy is entered by the teacher in the final column of the spreadsheet. As each group of pupils enters its data from the experiment (mass, temperatures and so on) the energy value is automatically generated on the spreadsheet. The final row of the spreadsheet averages the values of the data entered from each group, enabling the pupils to check the validity of their data and look for anomalies in the data set. The immediacy of the feedback from this enables pupils to act on the information rather than just acknowledge it. Results can be repeated, so as to improve the quality of the experimental process.

Collating results from the class experiment on the template is equivalent to the commonly drawn table on the blackboard or overhead projector. Each row of the spreadsheet represents an experiment from each group. This can be extended to take account of different types of food simply by adding an extra column and heading on the template. Comparisons of mass of food, food type or the work of each group add to the interactive nature of the task. The motivation of pupils generally increases when ICT is used in the classroom and this can be harnessed to good effect in this situation in order to maintain pupil interest during some of the more challenging aspects of the lesson.

Using a spreadsheet makes good use of a single computer in the classroom. It is not a strategy that requires large numbers of computers or a networked computer suite but one firmly based in the laboratory that enhances the practical science experience of the pupils. The key objective of the activity is to understand that food contains energy and to have an idea of the amount of energy contained in food. Their practical work and consequent calculations enable pupils to address this concept.

Looking for patterns in data

The importance of looking for patterns in data has been well documented as an activity that develops from the early years when children try to make sense of the world around them, to the more formal treatment and analysis of scientific patterns, relationships and trends as they move through their education. Access to ICT data-handling tools has enabled schools to move towards the vision set out by School Examination and Assessments Council (SEAC) in 1991, based on work by the Assessment of Performance Unit:

> It is reasonable to expect that a considerable proportion of school science should reflect such activity by providing pupils with opportunities to engage in the quest for patterns and relationships – and, also, to savour the excitement in this pursuit.
>
> (SEAC 1991)

The final phrase in this statement is interesting and relevant to the argument of using ICT to support data handling. Motivation is raised when computers are used in the classroom but, further, in work with large data sets mechanical analysis and manipulation can be time-consuming and cumbersome and obstruct the pursuit of understanding derived from the activity. Software can facilitate this activity, overcoming repetitive operations and allowing pupils to work with meaningful sample sizes and look for patterns in data where complex interaction between a number of variables may be evident.

Simple patterns can be observed by pupils but not as readily used as evidence to support predications and hypotheses. In these cases, instinct or other experience tends to be used by pupils in preference to empirical evidence collected from experiments and other sources. Adopting ICT data-handling techniques enables more immediate display of results, focusing pupils' attention on the emerging pattern in the data. An example of this approach is the use of a simple spreadsheet in a projectile investigation. Pupils are asked to suggest the optimum angle to achieve maximum range for firing a pellet from a catapult. An experiment is performed using an elastic band catapult placed on a ramp set up to fire paper pellets. As measurements of distance travelled by the pellet and angle of the ramp are collected they are immediately entered into the spreadsheet. The graph is generated as the data are entered and in turn is used to inform the next prediction of range. The feedback loop set up by this process is an effective way of structuring the pupils' thinking, with a clear focus on the relationship building up between angle and distance. There is still the usual element of surprise, however, when the range starts to decrease at angles greater than 45° (see Figure 7.3).

There are a number of similar examples in secondary school science where identifying the trend, pattern or relationship between variables is a vital element of the task. These include activities such as investigating heat loss and surface area/volume ratios, predicting values for unknown planets or elements from data set and identifying links between the carbohydrate, fat and energy contents of foods.

Angle	Prediction (cm)	Distance 1 (cm)	Distance 2 (cm)	Distance 3 (cm)	Average distance (cm)
0	0	0	0	0	0.0
10	10	4	5	5	4.7
20	10	8	6	9	7.7
30	12	15	10	11	12.0
40	17	20	18	16	18.0
50	21	16	19	18	17.7

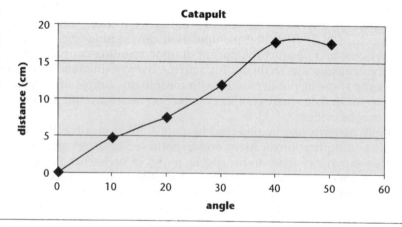

Figure 7.3   Catapult spreadsheet

Larger data sets offer a greater advantage in using ICT. Handling large amounts of data, such as environmental surveys, is a challenging and time-consuming task even for the most able pupils. Sorting and replotting data becomes more difficult as sample sizes increase beyond relatively small limits (plotting a class set of variation characteristics is close to the limit for most classes). However, entering large amounts of data into software is also an unproductive use of time and warrants the use of prepared data files for generic software or the use of dedicated software containing appropriate data sets.

The elements in the periodic table provide a rich source of data for pupils to use and may be best handled by software dedicated to the task. Essentially, data on each element is stored as a record in a database and, using appropriate software, these data can be searched, graphed and analysed for patterns and relationships. For example, plotting melting point against mass number begins to reveal cyclic patterns, which the pupils can link to the structure of the periodic table. It is difficult to envisage this type of pattern searching being done with all of the elements in the periodic table by manual methods. The example shown in Figure 7.4 uses a dedicated tool called Element Analyser (New Media), which has both analysis tools and a comprehensive data set, making this type of analysis straightforward.

An important aspect of pattern searching is to use knowledge and understanding to suggest relationships and trends and then try these out.

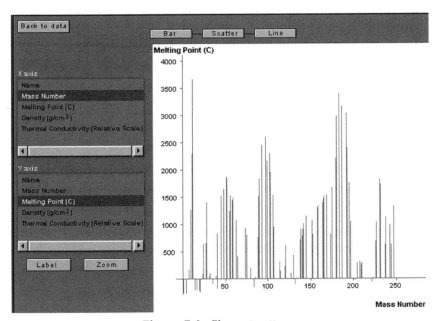

Figure 7.4   Element patterns

If pupils follow their own ideas there will inevitably be some null results but this is an essential element in this process and will be used by the pupils to inform their next prediction, provided the process of arriving at the output is not itself demotivating. The immediacy of ICT ensures that pupils are not bound up in a lengthy mechanical process and maintain their interest in the task.

Anomalous results are easily identifiable when patterns are observed in data sets and can be further investigated by pupils. There is scope for conditions to be set within software (conditional formulae or formatting in spreadsheets, for example) to highlight data that lie outside of an acceptable margin of error. This can be used to teach about the nature of data and sources of error in experiments to good effect.

Testing a hypothesis

Investigative work in science is based on pupils using evidence to support their ideas. Working from an initial model of understanding, the pupil suggests an explanation or hypothesis for the observed or described phenomena. Data collected from a primary or secondary source are then used to validate or disprove the hypothesis. Pupils are taught the scientific method (or a version of it), albeit in a constrained, and often trivial, context. Data handling has to be an integral part of this process. It is making sense of the data that challenges the pupil's original model of understanding. Patterns and correlations are sought between the key variables identified. This will normally be done using interpretation of graphical information. All the processes outlined above can be supported by the use of a spreadsheet.

Scenario 2

'So what do you think will affect the reaction time of a driver?' The teacher's opening gambit sets the task for the pupils. A brainstorm of factors will result from this statement, which are sifted to include only the plausible, and refined to give the measurable, such as gender, age, height, right-handed/left-handed (any variables can be included). Groups of pupils choose a factor and formulate their hypothesis: 'I think tall people will have slower reactions because the signal from their brain to their foot will have further to travel.' The task is then to set up an investigation collecting data to test their hypothesis.

The teacher and pupils now face a dilemma. The sample size within the groups will be small but needs to be of reasonable size to make the analysis realistic and valid. Collating class results using a spreadsheet increases the sample size from small group to whole class. Storage of information in electronic format provides the option to merge files from different classes or year groups, further increasing the sample size.

The spreadsheet is set up with the variables to be investigated as column headings, the data collection exercise being done as a class activity. Any method of measuring reaction time can be used, ranging from electronic timers to dropping and catching rulers (as in the example shown in Figure 7.5). The spreadsheet ensures that pupils repeat their experiment for each subject and average the results. Pupils will use a variety of strategies to interpret the data depending on their competence with ICT and understanding of data analysis techniques. The aim of the exercise is to consider the correlation of their chosen variable with the reaction time.

	A	C	D	E	F	G	H	I	J	K	L	M
1	Name	Weight (kg)	Eye colour	Age	R/L hand	Drop 1	Drop 2	Drop 3	Average	Time (s)	Sex	Pulse rate
3	Laura	46	grey	14	r	11	14	11	12.00	0.156	f	80
4	David	51	blue	14	r	11	10	10	10.33	0.145	m	70
5	Morag	49	brown	14	r	15	13	9	12.33	0.159	f	74
6	Rachel	38	green	14	l	12	11	12	11.67	0.154	f	78
7	Matthew	45	brown	14	r	13	14	10	12.33	0.159	m	74
8	Ben	56	brown	14	r	12	12	9	11.00	0.150	m	70
9	Rebecca	43	brown	13	r	15	13	9	12.33	0.159	f	84
10	Sally	38	blue	14	r	12	12	11	11.67	0.154	f	80
11	Karen	46	blue	14	r	12	12	10	11.33	0.152	f	80
12	Curtis	60	brown	14	r	15	14	10	13.00	0.163	m	76
13	Craig	51	blue	14	r	13	13	11	12.33	0.159	m	78
14	Darren	55	blue	13	l	10	9	8	9.00	0.135	m	72

Figure 7.5 Timing spreadsheet

Observations in classrooms have shown that pupils work at different levels in their approach to this task. At the simplest level, pupils tend to sort data into order and look for a regular increase or decrease in values. They try to match this to the order of reaction time, mimicking a manual approach to the task. The spreadsheet can support this approach with its sort and charting facilities and is a sensible starting point for development of data-handling skills, though the limitation of this approach soon becomes evident when working with more than one variable. It is straightforward to sort one column of data into ascending or descending order; comparing this to another variable and identifying a pattern will challenge many pupils. There is pedagogic reason in taking this approach in that it helps pupils to formalize the process of looking for the patterns. It also enables them to appreciate the difficulty in handling larger data sets in this way.

Pupils working at a higher level of competence will move directly to graphing the data. After selecting the columns of data to be graphed pupils will have to select the most appropriate type of graph suitable for displaying their data. This example, like most in science investigations, will require an *XY* plot to show the relationship between the variables. Most spreadsheets will direct pupils to a scatter graph as the preferred option for an *XY* plot. There is some confusion to be overcome as the term 'line graph' appears as an option on most spreadsheets. Pupils are familiar with this term, since 'draw a line graph' is the instruction normally given for an *XY* plot. However, the spreadsheet line graph will produce connected points from single data sets plotted against row number. Two sets of data will produce two lines, not an *XY* plot. This raises an important issue and is an example of where using ICT will confront pupils with choices and decisions requiring some rigour in thinking. In this example they will need to understand the terminology being used, the nature of the data they are dealing with and the reasons for the different graphical displays. These issues will need to be addressed by the teacher and provide rich opportunities for developing real understanding and insight, rather than a superficial treatment of the topic. Without a development of teaching in this area, teachers will continue to be presented with inappropriate choices of graph taken from the wide selection offered in the spreadsheet 'chart' options, such as the three-dimensional doughnut graph!

Having produced the scatter graph of points the pupils have to look for a pattern or correlation in the data. Opinion is divided here from a teaching perspective. The software can generate a trend line, again offering a series of options for the regression used. Many teachers prefer pupils to draw in their own line, seeing this as necessary to meet examination needs. The sensible solution is to use the most appropriate method for the needs of the pupils, depending on their ability and understanding. In the example given pupils would be expected to be able to describe the general trend

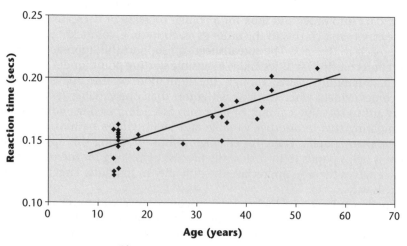

Figure 7.6   Reaction time graph

(for example, pupil comment might be 'As age increases the reaction time slows down') rather than to provide a mathematical treatment of the data. This reinforces the paradigm of having clear objectives for lessons in order to select and use the most effective and appropriate strategies and methods.

The data collected from investigations such as this will not always show clear patterns or fit to a mathematical expectation; there will often be a null result to the original hypothesis. Within the investigative process pupils are encouraged to evaluate their evidence and experimental procedure, which may mean reassessing the hypothesis and collecting more data. This can be added easily to the spreadsheet as an extra column. In the current example pupils decided to look at gender and pulse rate as secondary variables. This showed some refinement in their thinking and was a crucial stage in the learning process of this task. The provisional and interactive nature of ICT supports this iterative approach to learning and is supported by the dynamically expansive nature of the spreadsheet.

The spreadsheet has assisted the learning process throughout this example. Planning is aided by selecting variables, the tabular formats help pupils to organize their data collection and processing and graphing tools enable pupils to test their hypotheses and evaluate the investigation. Interestingly, this use of ICT has not removed the requirement for pupils to think, solve problems or use the data to develop their understanding. ICT has been used as a tool to enhance these activities.

Modelling

A model is some form of representation of a phenomenon or idea. Modelling is the process of formulating this representation (Gilbert 1993; Webb 1993). Such a representation can make use of a variety of formats from two-dimensional visual images to physical artefacts, and including the powerful medium of ICT. In science teaching, pupils' experiences, both in science lessons and outside the classroom, formulate their models of understanding. The teacher provides interventions to challenge pupils' ideas and move them towards a consensus model of understanding. Thus effective acquisition of knowledge has to involve the learner in formulating and testing ideas and this is not a one-way process. Bliss (1994) raises the potential of using models to promote learning ('models offer some possibility for the active engagement of pupils with ideas'), which highlights the interactive nature of the process. The inherent characteristics of the software that facilitates this process are its dynamic nature, interactivity, provisionality and iterative capability.

Computer-based models can bring together many of the positive attributes of other types of models. The visual impact can be stimulating and revealing, the interactivity encourages exploration, the provisionality (you can change it) allows the 'what would happen if?' factor to be explored and discovered. There will clearly be times when handling a physical model will have more impact or be more meaningful than an animation, but with ICT it is both faster and easier to try something out, change a variable and repeat actions. This has a very direct relevance to the process of learning science, particularly when working with more abstract phenomena, such as the flow of electricity. The graphical capability of ICT models can help the learner to see the concept from a more concrete perspective. The computer model will inevitably be based on mathematical models of the system being described. This does impose some limitation on how involved the pupil can be in the creation of the model and the function of modelling in the classroom. There is a distinction to be made between scientists' use of modelling, which is to facilitate the acquisition of new scientific knowledge, and the use of the model in the classroom, which is more concerned with enabling the pupils to appreciate and understand the scientific model (Sizmur and Ashby 1997).

Static modelling

In this approach changing a variable in the model will generate a new output. An example of this is shown using a spreadsheet model of vehicle stopping distances that calculates stopping distances at different speeds. The calculation for stopping distance is linked to two variables relating to the driver's reaction time and the efficiency of the vehicle's brakes. Changing the value of either of these variables causes a resultant change to the stopping distance, reflected by the graph of stopping distance against speed. In this way pupils can investigate other effects, such as driver tiredness, alcohol consumption and road conditions. The spreadsheet model offers opportunities for pupil interactions on a number of levels. In the example shown in Figure 7.7, the pupils are likely to change the data and observe the resultant effects. There will also be occasions when the pupils set up their own models as a learning activity. It is the decision of the teacher at which level the pupils will operate and how much of the underlying mechanisms and calculations is available to the pupils, which promotes independent and differentiated learning (Carson 1997).

Dynamic modelling

In this type of model an iterative calculation is used to model a system as a function of time. This type of approach is particularly useful for analysing motion, electrical systems and population dynamics. In the example shown, simple harmonic motion is investigated by altering the initial parameters, such as damping coefficient and amplitude. From a teaching point of view this spreadsheet could be used on a number of different levels according to pupil needs and intended learning outcomes: as a

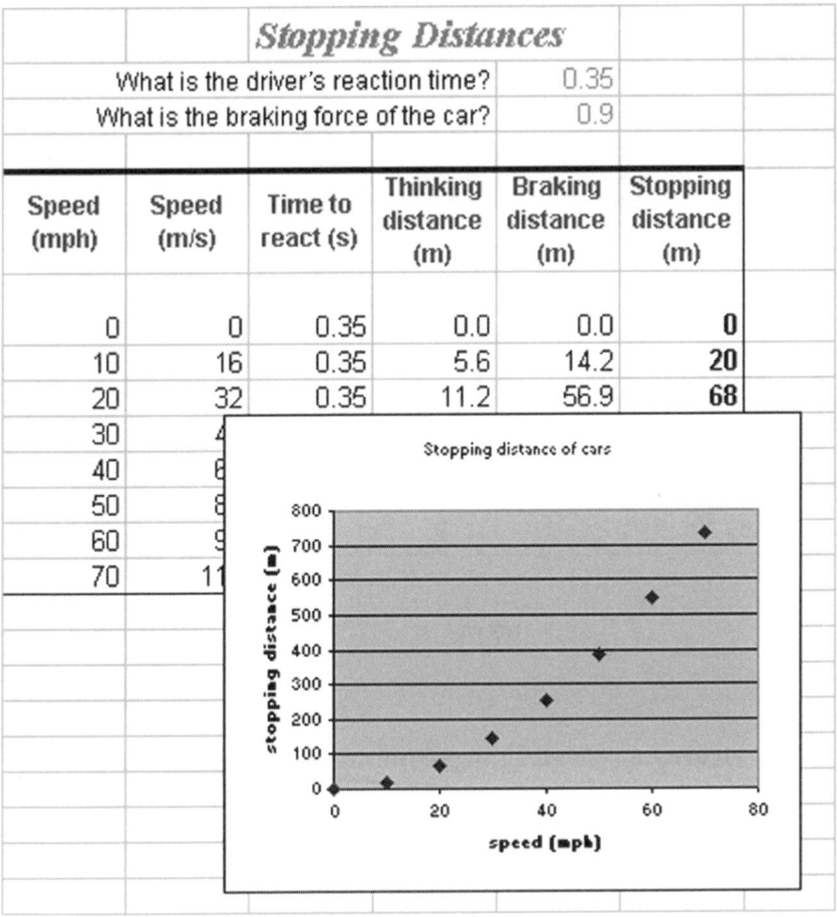

		Stopping Distances				
	What is the driver's reaction time?			0.35		
	What is the braking force of the car?			0.9		
Speed (mph)	Speed (m/s)	Time to react (s)	Thinking distance (m)	Braking distance (m)	Stopping distance (m)	
0	0	0.35	0.0	0.0	0	
10	16	0.35	5.6	14.2	20	
20	32	0.35	11.2	56.9	68	
30						
40						
50						
60						
70	1					

Figure 7.7   Investigating stopping distances

demonstration tool, as an interactive model or as an exercise for the pupils to create. This mode of use progresses with pupil capability and understanding of the underlying scientific principles and the use of the spreadsheet. Each level is a valid mode of study and teaching. Exploring the model in an interactive way, investigating the effect of increasing the damping coefficient, for example, develops pupils' awareness of the interdependence of variables and their effects on the system. At the final level, the pupils would need to understand the physics and mathematics of the system and how to use spreadsheet formulae, graphs and conditions in order to be able to construct the model. This level of sophistication indicates pupil depth of understanding of the system and the activity is a powerful learning tool and experience in itself.

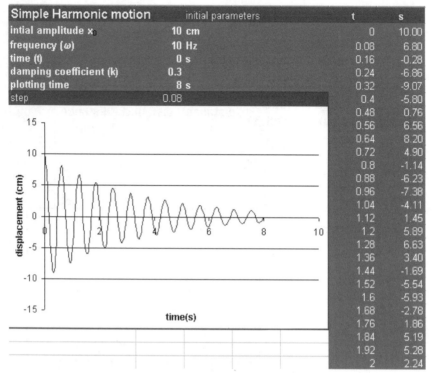

Simple Harmonic motion	initial parameters	t	s
intial amplitude x_0	10 cm	0	10.00
frequency (ω)	10 Hz	0.08	6.80
time (t)	0 s	0.16	-0.28
damping coefficient (k)	0.3	0.24	-6.86
plotting time	8 s	0.32	-9.07
step	0.08	0.4	-5.80
		0.48	0.76
		0.56	6.56
		0.64	8.20
		0.72	4.90
		0.8	-1.14
		0.88	-6.23
		0.96	-7.38
		1.04	-4.11
		1.12	1.45
		1.2	5.89
		1.28	6.63
		1.36	3.40
		1.44	-1.69
		1.52	-5.54
		1.6	-5.93
		1.68	-2.78
		1.76	1.86
		1.84	5.19
		1.92	5.28
		2	2.24

Figure 7.8 Modelling simple harmonic motion with damping

The principles of dynamic modelling are not restricted to the domain of the spreadsheet. Specific modelling environments have been developed that make use of these techniques. The Dynamic Modelling System, a software package for the BBC Microcomputer, was used as part of the Nuffield advanced physics course for many years. More recently modelling became an integral part of the post-16 advancing physics course, and this features a dynamic modelling environment called Modellus, which includes a sophisticated and enhanced graphical interface with different windows representing different elements of the system.

Most specific packages dedicated to particular topics make the mathematical principles transparent and focus on the scenario of the model. This may result in a qualitative treatment of relationships, which will be sufficient for most teaching for the 11 to 16 age group. Predator–prey relationships are a classic example of such a situation, where interaction can only be achieved using software, particularly when looking at trends over a number of generations. It is possible to use a spreadsheet to model predator–prey relationships using iterative calculations (Carson 1996), but even when limited to small numbers of species, this requires complex mathematics to model the system accurately and is best handled with software specifically written for the task. An alternative solution to the iterative treatment of problems is to use an object-oriented approach to building the model. In this technique rules are assigned to objects that govern their interaction with other objects over a period or time. The output from the interactions can be displayed as a graph, enabling pupils to seeing the resulting effects of the interactions.

There have been several attempts to devise generic modelling software engines using this object-oriented approach. The advantage is that, although the underlying rule is mathematical, usually a probability function, the software can be made to interpret rules set by pupils using simple language-driven statements such as 'foxes eat rabbits'. The statements are then translated by the software to produce the mathematical model. The potential in this is that the activity becomes a true modelling exercise for pupils, rather than a simulation of a modelling experience. The work of Papert using LOGO programming environments in the 1980s made many claims for the learning gains from such adventures (Papert 1980). Unfortunately, there is little evidence of a significant impact of this approach or indeed much provision of such software in the mainstream science curriculum.

Scenario 3

In physics modules for pupils aged 14 to 16, calculating the cost of electrical energy is a relevant activity covering energy conservation issues and helping to develop an understanding of quantities and relationships in current electricity. Typically this would be done as a whole-class lesson, with teacher input and pupil practice and with a limited number of calculations, depending on the ability of the class, perhaps with some additional reference to electricity bills. The use of the simple spreadsheet model can extend this to a more investigative and active learning experience.

In the ICT-led approach pupils work in groups on the task, perhaps in a network room, creating their own spreadsheet model or adapting a prepared template. The spreadsheet is used as a framework or template for repeating calculations. A decision on the level of pupil input is part of teacher lesson preparation and will be based on pupil ability and the key objectives for the lesson. This is a science lesson but offers an opportunity for the development of ICT skills and capability, with appropriate planning and management by the teacher.

The template will contain all the relevant column headings, providing a structure for the pupils to develop their model. Constructing this model impels the pupils to understand the concepts and formulae involved. The template prompts pupils to break the problem down into steps and

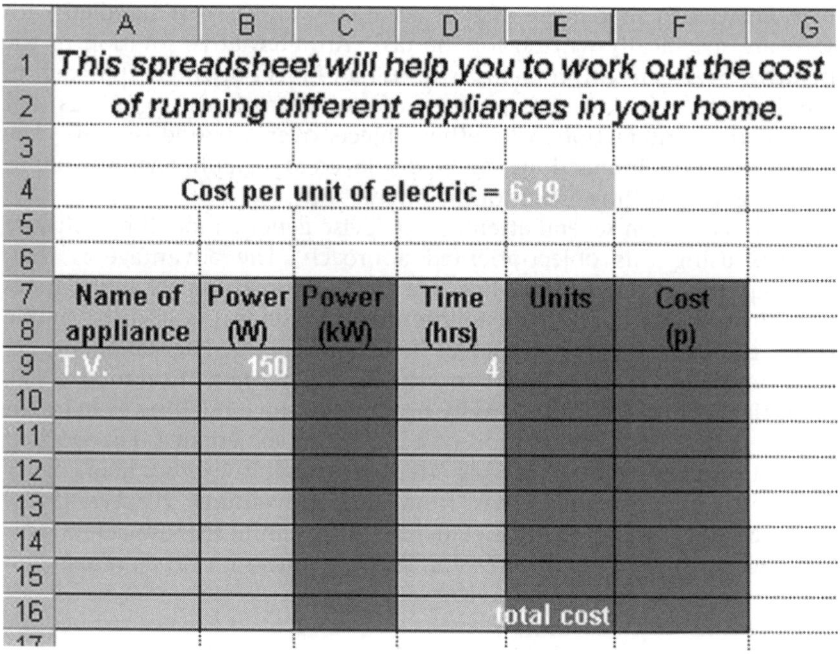

	A	B	C	D	E	F	G
1	This spreadsheet will help you to work out the cost						
2	of running different appliances in your home.						
3							
4	Cost per unit of electric =				6.19		
5							
6							
7	Name of	Power	Power	Time	Units	Cost	
8	appliance	(W)	(kW)	(hrs)		(p)	
9	T.V.	150		4			
10							
11							
12							
13							
14							
15							
16					total cost		
17							

Figure 7.9 Electrical energy calculations

enables them to see how the calculation is done, as opposed to being presented with an answer to the problem and slotting numbers into the function. For example, the raw data of appliance power in watts is converted into kilowatts using a simple conversion factor in column C of the spreadsheet shown in Figure 7.9. Through working out and entering this formula the pupils understand the underlying principles. The data are used in subsequent columns to calculate units in kWh and finally the cost of the using the appliance, which is linked to a cell containing the electricity cost per unit.

Once the model has been constructed the pupils can use it in their investigations. A typical approach to this might be to compare different scenarios – the difference between the overall cost per month for a family of four in winter and summer, for example. This can be extrapolated using the framework to look at the overall demands on energy consumption during these periods. This adds to the realism of the topic and provides a meaningful and familiar context for the pupils, moving the experience from a numerical exercise to an engaging activity with social and economic importance. A simple but effective example of static spreadsheet modelling enhances the science topic being covered.

Conclusion

This chapter has considered the role of ICT in data handling in science teaching. The importance of this area of learning in science is in supporting and developing the related processes, such as organization and manipulation of data. The subsequent access to analysis and graphing techniques leads to more effective interpretation of the data sets, enabling pupils to recognize patterns and trends in their results.

Scaife and Wellington (1993) refer to the in-built benefits provided by computers: being able to collect and store large amounts of data to perform rapid calculations on data and to process and display the data. These features all relate to data-handling capability. This has to be harnessed, as they indicate, in terms of the learner, not those of the technology.

These approaches to teaching cannot be applied in isolation and without consideration of basic teaching principles. The methodologies discussed are strategies that can be employed by teachers in appropriate situations with a considered and systematically planned approach. This is not unique to the area of data handling but is perhaps even more important than in some other uses of ICT, as it is likely to be just one aspect of many, not the total focus of the lesson. The approach of choosing appropriate strategies to meet science learning objectives is actively promoted in UK schools as the basis of the recent government teaching training initiative for serving teachers (TTA 1999) and as part of the National Curriculum for trainee teachers (DfEE 1998). It is encouraging that these directives see the use of ICT as a teaching strategy to support subject objectives and highlight the need for teachers to understand the role that ICT can play in enhancing subject learning. This has implications for planning, teaching and assessment. ICT is not a 'bolt-on' solution or a panacea to solve all the shortcomings in teaching; it has to be an integral part of the lesson, curriculum-focused and meeting learning needs to be successful. Organizing this resource in the classroom, particularly in the science laboratory, calls for decisions to be made as to the most effective methods and may demand new approaches and roles for the teacher. The use of the spreadsheet to collate results makes good use of a single computer in the classroom, for example, whereas using a model to explore scientific phenomena will require small group or individual access to computers. The demands on pupils' ICT capability will need to be addressed during the planning. The skill levels for creating a model are much greater than those for using a preparatory piece of software dedicated to the task. This may mean liaison with other departments within the school or an intensive skills-based lesson, both of which might be difficult to achieve. Assessment of the learning outcomes needs to be matched to lesson objectives and not to be diverted or masked by the ICT content of the lesson. The output from software is not always a good indicator of pupils' science understanding, and this calls for more creative

assessment methods, which take greater account of the process and thinking undertaken by the pupils. I have observed increasing use of presentations by pupils and peer teaching activities planned by teachers as
imaginative methods of assessment.

These are not issues to be treated superficially, and they deserve priority
in teacher development programmes. Unfortunately, too often the technology comes before the teaching, shifting the emphasis and focus of the
lesson. Teachers and educators should be mindful of the ease with which
the use of technology in the classroom can subsume the main objectives
and purpose of the lesson. 'Thinking about using computers in education
means thinking about education not computers' (Ellis quoted in Coupland
et al. 1988: 21) is a pertinent statement that should be printed as a government warning on all educational software and hardware.

References

Bliss, J. (1994) From mental models to modelling, in H. Mellar, J. Bliss, R. Boohan,
    J. Ogborn and C. Tomsett (eds) *Learning with Artificial Worlds: Computer Based
    Modelling in the Curriculum.* London: Falmer Press.
Carson, S. (1996) Foxes and rabbits – and a spreadsheet, *School Science Review*,
    78(283): 21–7.
Carson, S. (1997) The use of spreadsheets in science, *School Science Review*, 79(287):
    69–80.
Coupland, J., Benzie, D., Butcher, P., Liebling, H. and Spurgeon, P. (1988) *The Rain-
    bow Project.* Coventry: MESU.
DfEE (1998) *Teaching: High Status, High Standards. Requirements for Courses of Initial
    Teacher Training.* Circular 4/98. London: The Stationery Office.
DfEE and QCA (1999) *Science: The National Curriculum for England.* London: The
    Stationery Office.
Gilbert, J. K. (ed.) (1993) *Models and Modelling in Science.* Hatfield: Association for
    Science Education.
Millar, R. (1996) A science curriculum for public understanding, *School Science
    Review*, 77(280): 7–18.
Milner, B. (1986) Why teach science and why to all?, in J. Nellist and B. Nicholl
    (eds) *The ASE Science Teachers' Handbook.* London: Hutchinson.
Papert, S. (1980) *Mindstorms: Children, Computers and Powerful Ideas.* New York:
    Harvester.
Scaife, J. and Wellington, J. J. (1993) *Information Technology in Science and Technology
    Education.* Buckingham: Open University Press.
SEAC (1991) *Patterns and Relationships in School Science.* London: HMSO.
Sizmur, S. and Ashby, J. (1997) *Introducing Scientific Concepts to Children.* Slough:
    NFER.
TTA (1999) *The Use of ICT in Subject Teaching.* London: TTA Publications.
Webb, M. (1993) Computer-based modelling in school science, *School Science
    Review*, 74(269): 33–47.

Part V

An International Perspective

8

THE APPROACH TO ICT IN SCIENCE EDUCATION IN THE NETHERLANDS

Ton Ellermeijer

Editor's introduction

The earlier chapters in this book are all written in the context of the use of ICT in the UK. This chapter is different, since it not only describes the use of ICT in another country, the Netherlands, but also aims to provide an overview of how another country has approached the development and use of ICT. The basic software applications relevant to science education remain the same but the ways in which these have been used, and the differences in the strategic approach taken, provide a complementary view to that provided elsewhere in this book.

The Dutch school system

In Dutch schools the number of subjects studied is high. In the lower secondary level pupils have 14 subjects and in the upper level it ranges from 9 to 14. At lower secondary level (age 12–15) science is divided into biology and a combination of physics and chemistry. At the upper level (age 16–18) pupils choose a combination of subjects called a profile or sector. There are two profiles with an emphasis on science. In these profiles, science is divided into biology, physics and chemistry. About half the pupils in upper level secondary schools choose one of the science profiles.

At the upper level of secondary education there is a movement towards more individual learning. This often happens outside scheduled lessons, in what are called 'studyhouses', an important development for education in the Netherlands. Contact hours with teachers are replaced by independent work with, or without, the help of a teacher.

The context: computers in Dutch schools

Computers in the Netherlands first started to be used in education in the early 1980s. From 1985 to 1988, a government-funded project called NIVO (New Information Technology in Secondary Education) donated IBM-compatible computers to schools. Many schools bought additional computers and so the IBM PC became the standard in secondary schools. In addition to this hardware, schools received a basic package of software and some in-service training.

At the lower level of secondary education, compulsory computer science courses were introduced. From 1993, specific science-related ICT attainment targets were added to these requirements, which required pupils to be skilled in using the computer for acquiring and processing science-related data, and in using the computer to understand processes via simulations and modelling. At the upper level of secondary education, the government chose to promote the use of information technology within curriculum subjects, rather than introducing a separate computer science course. Physics was the first of these subjects. Schools received extra budgets to acquire the necessary equipment and a national project for in-service training of physics teachers was conducted. From that time on, data logging and modelling became popular in the schools, first in physics and then in chemistry and biology. Teacher training (CPD) via INSET courses was one of the main reasons for the success of this initiative. (Recently a pilot project has been started to investigate whether synchronous distance learning techniques are helpful in providing in-service training (Ellermeijer *et al.* 2001).)

In considering the introduction of modelling into the curriculum, it became evident that the physics programme was overloaded. For that reason, in 1994 the government mandated that online measurements, data processing and modelling must be assessed as part of school-based practical exams, rather than in written examinations. Until the end of the 1990s, computers were used in science mostly for practical work or investigations. The data logging took place in science laboratories and the modelling in schools' computer rooms. Schools also began to use other software packages, such as simulation programs.

Recently the increasing use of the Internet, together with a growing interest in individual learning, has resulted in new types of computer use. The Dutch government has promoted the use of a central Internet provider, called KennisNet (http://www.kennisnet.nl), although schools are still free to decide for themselves whether or not they wish to use this service. KennisNet has created a large intranet for schools and related institutions. Every school connected now has access to a large network of computers. This means that computers in school laboratories, computer rooms and the studyhouses now have access to a wide range of media libraries. Pupils can access these sources on the Internet and use the data for their school work. The experience of learning in the studyhouse has led teachers to set more open-ended activities and so consulting sources via the Internet is now important.

Currently only one science-based project is available via KennisNet, called Virtual Labs. In this project, measurements using digital video clips of science topics and activities using computer-based modelling are the main activities. Using these resources, teachers are able to create individual learning activities, which can be accessed by pupils in the studyhouse.

Most schools have an internal network connected to the Internet via KennisNet. KennisNet connects schools with libraries, museums, the Educational Broadcast Company (Teleac/NOT) and other educational institution. Several universities have special sites specifically devoted to secondary education. A new facility is the ability to access the Internet in several places within a school. Science teachers are able to use the Internet for a range of useful information sources, such as relevant newsgroups, gaining information from universities and accessing government information.

Coach as a major factor in ICT and science education

In the Netherlands, unlike the UK, there was pressure to produce a software environment that would integrate the features of data-logging and modelling software. This led to the development of the first Coach software in 1988. This software, known as IP-Coach 2, provided support for a data-logging interface including powerful analysis tools, and also provided software modelling facilities. Over the years, other valuable tools have been added to the environment, such as control activities and the capacity to analyse digital video. The Coach 4 environment, still a DOS-based software package, became the *de facto* standard in Dutch schools, together with the hardware for data logging. Because of this situation, publishers, curriculum committees and teacher training institutes could all concentrate on making the best use of this environment, enabling schools and teachers to receive consistent and strong support for their work in this area. Because of its versatile character Coach has come to be used not only in physics, but also in chemistry, biology and technology education.

While the Coach 4 environment was the subject of some international interest, the present environment, Coach 5, has attracted considerably more international attention. Coach 5 is an activity-based environment based on a new concept, made possible by the Windows environment. Activities are grouped into projects. In this way a developer (such as a teacher or textbook author) is able to create, for example, a close link to a chapter in a book. Of course, teachers and curriculum developers want to develop a variety of ways for pupils to become involved with the learning content. Coach 5 gives opportunities to build a learning environment with multimedia activities that include:

- texts with explanations and instructions of activities;
- pictures to illustrate experiments and equipment;
- video clips to illustrate phenomena or to make video-based measurements;
- (measured) data presented in forms of graphs, tables, meters or digital values;
- models (graphical or numerical), which theoretically describe science phenomena;
- programs to control devices and control systems;
- links to Internet sites to give access to extra resources for pupils.

This means that in addition to all the tools for science and technology education, teachers and developers have at their disposal powerful authoring tools to prepare activities for their pupils. They can select and prepare texts, graphs, videos and measurement settings and choose the right level according to the age and skill level of their pupils. In this way Coach 5 can be adapted for pupils and students ranging from age 10 up to undergraduate level. Coach 5 is not only used in science and technology but also has applications in mathematics education. It is used by almost all Dutch secondary schools, and those in many European countries, although the uptake in these countries differs considerably. Coach 5 has been translated into over ten languages. Up-to-date information on the Coach environment can be obtained on the website: www.cma.science.uva.nl/english. A demonstration version can be downloaded from this site.

Coach 5

Nowadays schools use a variety of interfaces to support data logging and control activities. In biology and environmental studies, data loggers such as CBL and Ecolog are popular. To avoid the need for teachers and pupils to have to use different software packages, Coach 5 supports a variety of hardware platforms, such as:

- CoachLab interfaces, distributed by CMA, a foundation affiliated with the AMSTEL Institute;
- LEGO DACTAfi Control products (including RCX);
- Texas Instruments CBL! and CBR!;
- Fourier Systems EcoLog.

All these interfaces or data loggers are handled in the same way by the software. Even an activity developed for one interface can easily be changed for another platform.

Most activities are based on specific tools for collecting or generating data, such as data loggers or data video analysis. A measurement activity (time-based or event-based measurement) enables pupils to collect data on-line and off-line using sensors. During the measurements, data can be presented in graphs, tables and meters or displayed as digital values. Experiments are easy to set up using drag-and-drop sensor icons and a library with calibrated sensors and actuators is available.

A data video activity allows the collection of position and time data from digital video clips by clicking on the location of the items of interest in each frame of the digital movie. These data can be plotted and used for further analysis (similar to the Motion software described in Chapter 6). Data video enables pupils to study events that occur outside the classroom. The user has control of a range of factors, such as the number of data-points from each frame. While reading data from graphs it is possible to view the relevant video sequence simultaneously.

A control activity offers several modes of programming with increasing levels of difficulty. These modes are a manual control mode, an instruction mode, a micro-world programming mode and a free programming mode. The environment is used to create programs to control systems from fixed models (such as crossroads) and models built from elements (for example, LEGO DACTA models) right up to student-designed models controlled by the CoachLab interface. Experienced students can program freely or create their own commands in the Coach language. While a program is running, all the inputs and outputs can be monitored. Pupils studying technology are able to explore control systems using this software. The control environment also allows the creation of automated measuring systems; for example, controlling the flow of liquid for a titration while measuring with a pH sensor.

A modelling activity offers an environment to create numerical models of complex real-life phenomena. For creating models, two types of editors are available, a graphical and a text editor. The graphical editor was developed to make the first stage of modelling activities easier. Then a student might decide to switch to the text mode to add to or change the model. Based on the given numerical model, iterative calculations are performed. The model results can then be compared with experimental data. Once the model has been created, it is easy to modify its results by changing parameters, and this can be used by students to test their hypothesis and make links between the real experiment and the theoretical model.

The software tools available make it possible for the same array of tools to be available for the analysis of data gathered via data video or modelling as is normally available for measurements collected via data logging.

The Resonance project: a case study

The Resonance project is an example of a Coach 5 multimedia project that involves many different types of activities, and it demonstrates the rich possibilities of such an environment. A combination of text, pictures, digital video clips, computer measurement, control, modelling and web technology is applied in this project, whose objectives are to:

- study concepts such as natural frequency, forced oscillations and resonance;
- investigate the natural frequency of different objects;
- investigate forced oscillations;
- investigate the problem of resonance in bridges;
- compare theory with experiment using the modelling environment.

The Coach environment allows the creation of multimedia activities, including laboratory-based activities and curriculum materials, using the Author program. As a teacher or curriculum developer you can insert your own instructions, along with images and even video clips. It is possible to identify different modes of use, from 'Junior Fixed', which gives pupils access to only a few necessary controls, to 'Junior Flexible' and 'Junior Own Lab'. Finally, a 'Senior Student' mode allows students to use Coach as an open set of tools.

The Resonance project consists of seven activities and a pupil guide:

- *Activity 1: Video clips.* Introduction. In 1940, four months after being completed, the Tacoma Narrows Bridge in the state of Washington, USA, was destroyed by a 40 mile per hour wind. Pupils can see the original video clips of this event and are asked to answer questions. This activity is used as an activity to trigger discussion leading to an interest in the 'Resonance phenomenon'.
- *Activity 2: Measurement.* Natural frequency. This activity is aimed at exploring what is meant by the natural frequency of an object. Measurements are made using a sound sensor to collect data on a vibrating tuning fork. Fourier analysis of the data can be carried out to determine the frequency of the sound.
- *Activity 3: Measurement.* Spring oscillations. What is the natural frequency of an oscillating 'spring–mass' system? In this activity the

natural frequency of such a system can be found by attaching a force sensor to the oscillating spring.

- *Activity 4: Control.* Forced oscillations. We can force a magnet hanging on a spring to oscillate by passing the spring through a coil carrying an alternating current. This is done with the help of a program prepared in the control activity. When the frequency of the forced oscillations matches the system's natural frequency then resonance occurs. Pupils can also observe the beats when the driving frequency is slightly different from the resonant frequency.
- *Activity 5: Video clips, web pages.* Resonating bridges. Can you explain why the Tacoma Narrows Bridge collapsed? Pupils can watch videos of model bridge demonstrations to help them to answer this question (Fuller *et al.* 1982).
- *Activity 6: Modelling.* With the help of the modelling environment the phenomenon of forced oscillations can be explored. First the model is explained and then values are taken for the different quantities from the real experiment. With the model, simulations can be carried out by changing, for instance, the period of the driving force. In this way data from the real experiment can be matched with data generated by the model. These data can be displayed on in the same graph.
- *Activity 7: Video clips.* Assessment. Do you understand the concept of resonance? Check your knowledge by watching video clips and answering questions. The video clips show different resonance phenomena, such as Ella Fitzgerald shattering a wine glass, or the earthquake in Kobe, Japan.

The seven activities identified above illustrate the ways in which the Coach 5 software environment can be used by curriculum developers, or an individual teacher, to bring together text, images and sound with data-logging and modelling software. It is the integration of these teaching tools, and the ability to customize them for a particular teaching situation, that makes the system so powerful.

Future developments

The development of the Coach environment has been an ongoing project since 1986, driven by classroom experience, educational research and developments in technology. In the next few years extensions are planned to make better use of the Internet to facilitate more collaborative work between pupils and between teachers; for example, supporting the exchange of experimental results and lesson plans. But the vital message for the Dutch education system is one that should concern all science teachers: to take up the challenge to ensure that the new technologies do not become an end in themselves but instead serve the needs of science education.

References

Ellermeijer, A. L., Landheer, B. and Molenaar, P. P. M. (1996) Teaching mechanics through interactive video and a microcomputer-based laboratory, in R. F. Tinker (ed.) *Microcomputer-based Labs: Educational Research and Standards.* Amsterdam: Springer-Verlag.

Ellermeijer, A. L., Dorenbos, V. J. and Mulder, C.H.T. (2001) In-service training of science teachers with synchronous distance learning, Paper presented at the ESERA conference, Thessaloniki, August (www.science.uva.nl/research/amstel/dl).

Fuller, R. F., Zollman, D. and Campbell, T. (1982) *The Puzzle of Tacoma Narrows Bridge Collapse*, Videodisc. Chichester: Wiley Educational Software.

Part VI

What Next?

9

INTEGRATING ICT INTO SCIENCE EDUCATION AND THE FUTURE

Laurence Rogers

When microcomputers first became available in education at an economic cost in the early 1980s, science teachers, with their general experience in managing technical equipment, were well placed to take advantage of the facilities offered by the new technology. In particular, the BBC Micro-computer, adopted widely in schools, was accompanied by a very friendly programming language, BBC BASIC, which encouraged many teachers with mathematical and scientific skills to become amateur programmers and create their own software serving a variety of educational needs. Of special interest to science teachers was the provision of an internal circuit for measuring voltage inputs through an 'analogue port', which could be readily put to use for measurements in the school laboratory. Coupled with rudimentary sensors, it became possible to measure temperature, light, motion, voltage and other physical quantities with a precision and repetition only possible hitherto with expensive laboratory instruments beyond the limits of school budgets. With this facility, data logging was born and computers found an early welcome in science education.

Since those pioneering days, not only has data logging developed in sophistication, but the broad range of software applications described in this book has emerged, serving a wide variety of needs in science education. The wealth of software now available has eliminated the need for amateur programming and with the general reduction in the technical expertise necessary for using programs, the vast majority of teachers, and their students, can now engage as consumers of the technology. But how does the technology serve the curriculum? Many of the early pioneers were driven by a mixture of an intrinsic interest in the technology with a vision of software tools as calculating, instructional and visual aids for tackling specific science teaching needs. At the present time in Britain, following a succession of national initiatives, the role of ICT is now regarded as fundamental to the modern curriculum in all subjects. Despite this government positioning on ICT, its integration into schemes of work in schools appears to be a slow process. A possible reason for this is that teachers possess only a partial understanding of the potential contribution of ICT to the processes of teaching and learning. To discuss this contribution in greater depth, we need to begin by considering some fundamental aspects: the aims of teaching science and the different types of learning involved in science.

Teaching and learning

The general aims of teaching in any subject area are well rehearsed in curricular statements and syllabuses for public examinations. Jean Underwood provides a succinct statement of key educational goals implicit in such statements: 'The primary responsibility of the teacher is to encourage the cognitive development of the child, to ensure the retention, understanding and active use of knowledge and skills' (Underwood 1994: 2). To consider how ICT can contribute to achieving these goals in science requires us to think about the different types of learning implicit in this statement. Science teachers will readily identify with a vocation to promote the learning of concepts, knowledge and skills. Each type of learning requires different teaching approaches, which are best understood by considering three models of learning.

Concepts

A 'constructivist' model is most appropriate for describing the learning of concepts. New experiences are interpreted in the light of previously acquired knowledge; new ideas are assimilated when they conform to previous cognitive schemas (Underwood 1994: 3). Concept development is central to science teaching, such as when teaching topics like energy, forces and particles. To develop concepts and to counter misconceptions, students need to be encouraged to think for themselves. Their ideas need to be made explicit and challenged by new experiences. ICT tools have great potential to encourage this style of learning, which requires responses to the student's individual needs. Software can present many

choices and alternatives to the student, providing an interactive experience well suited to individual exploration. These ideas were explored in
Chapter 6 on multimedia, where the visual, dynamic and interactive facilities provided a tool to support students as they explored issues such as
terminal velocity or the kinetic theory of matter. There is still an important role for the teacher as a challenger, target setter and trouble shooter,
but in view of the reality that students cannot normally expect the
undivided attention of their teacher, some of this role is usefully delegated
to software.

Skills and their application

An 'apprenticeship' model helps to describe the learning of skills. The
essence of this model is that learning occurs through imitation and the
acquisition of cultural traditions. The study of science requires specific
skills, such as observation, manipulation of apparatus, measurement,
recording, graphing and so on, as well as generic skills, such as communication and presentation. In order to apply such skills in a meaningful way,
learners also require a procedural understanding, which is, essentially, the
thinking that needs to accompany the exercise of the skill (Gott and
Duggan 1995: 26). This type of understanding encompasses, for example,
identifying variables, ideas about fair testing, repeatability and accuracy of
measurements and interpreting graphs. The effect of ICT is to change the
relative importance of a range of skills used in science; for example, data
logging can diminish the mechanical aspects of collecting data but can
enhance the use of graphs for the interpretation of data. Tutorial programs
can usefully facilitate the practice and reinforcement of skills, aspects of
learning that are implicit in an apprenticeship model. Unfortunately,
there is a training cost to this benefit, in that ICT also adds to the overall
skills requirement in the classroom in respect of the operational skill
needed to use software and the computer itself.

Knowledge

A 'behaviourist' model is suitable for considering the learning of knowledge in the form of large bodies of structured material. In science there is a
multitude of facts and information upon which concepts and skills
depend. For example, facts about the physical and chemical properties of
elements are a prerequisite to the development of ideas embodied in the
periodic table of elements. Such knowledge requires storage in readiness
for recall but no reconstruction in the head of the learner. This type of
learning is described by a behaviourist model that requires learners to
modify their response to the learning process until the 'correct' knowledge
is recalled. Clearly ICT provides numerous means of conveying informational knowledge and potentially usurps this aspect of traditional

teaching. So powerful is ICT in giving access to large volumes of information, skills of searching, selecting and validating data need to assume a more prominent role in relation to the use of the Internet in science teaching.

Fitness for purpose

In order to develop a rationale for deciding when and how to use ICT in science, it is important to recognize the different types of learning described here, since, for any learning activity, the purpose of the activity must be informed by the type of learning involved. When we are clear about the learning purpose we can use an appropriate learning model to help to identify the suitable usage of ICT. A particular ICT method should be chosen and evaluated with reference to the learning purpose. As with the planning of any lesson, it is important to have a clear idea of the learning objectives of the science lesson.

To progress to a consideration of the appropriateness of an ICT method, it is necessary to identify the benefits of the method compared with conventional (non-ICT) alternatives. This process is sometimes more subtle than appears at first because beneficial outcomes are usually dependent on factors other than the type of software chosen. In particular, the teaching approach and aspects of the previous training of students have a strong influence on outcomes (see Rogers and Wild 1996). A useful way of developing this point is to distinguish between the 'properties' of software features and the 'potential benefits' to learning that might flow from each feature. Table 9.1 summarizes a number of examples of properties and benefits for various types of software used in science education, many of which have been discussed in more detail in earlier chapters. For further examples, see Newton and Rogers 2001.

The properties column of this table lists some of the 'good' things that software can do, but, as such, none of them explicitly describes a benefit in terms of learning. It is appropriate to use the term 'properties' because the statements are merely descriptors of *what* the software can do. On the other hand, the second column attempts to identify aspects of learning that may be considered beneficial, and these depend upon *how* the software is employed. Such benefits must be qualified as 'potential' because a particular property can only deliver a benefit if it matches an identified teaching purpose and is exploited in a suitable context of activity.

To illustrate this distinction, consider, for example, the property of automatic plotting in graphing software; this can be considered as offering no benefit at all if the student is thereby deprived of learning basic plotting skills. However, the same property enables students to plot many graphs in succession, allowing the repetition of an experiment under different conditions or exploring data by plotting alternative versions of the graph.

Table 9.1 Examples of properties and benefits of different types of software

Properties of software	Potential benefits
Information systems	
Search engines facilitate versatile and speedy searching	• Encourages attention to detail of content • Encourages use of science process skills • Develops search and selection skills • Promotes classification skills
Publishing tools	
Text is easily modified using editing tools	• Pupils develop thoughts in their own way • Ease of change encourages reflection and refinement • Remodelling text encourages thought
Visual aids	
Use of colour, varied fonts and text sizes as visual cues, emphasizing the structure of information	• Helps to focus attention and evaluation of information • Assists comprehension
Simulations	
'Virtual' experiments are possible	• Provides safe alternative to dangerous, difficult, expensive or specialized experiments • 'Clean' data builds confidence in analysis • Visualization of difficult concepts
Graphing tools	
Plotting process is automatic	• Low skill level required • Improved plotting accuracy • Time saved
Data logging	
'Real time' reporting	• Interactive • Encourages thinking about data

Exploited in this way, automatic plotting enables students to search for patterns in data, compare sets of data and study the effect of variables. For less able students, who might normally struggle to produce an accurate graph, automatic plotting can boost their confidence in using the graph as a tool for visualizing and interpreting data, see chapter 2.

Many software applications enable tasks to be completed more rapidly than through conventional means, thus offering a time bonus. For the time bonus to be a benefit, the choice of tasks needs careful thought by the teacher. Sometimes, as suggested above, it is useful to use the time by repeating the experiment several times. Often, with 'real-time' data logging, students can use the time to make more careful observations of the experiment while data collection is in progress. As a general principle it is useful for students to develop a culture of questioning and observation during experiments so that the time bonus is not wasted.

Interactivity is an implicit theme in certain software properties. The overt indicators of interactivity are software features that offer choices to the user and appear to customize the behaviour of the program to the user's responses. It is important to recognize that genuine interactivity requires the learner to be engaged (Wills 1996, cited in Stoney and Wild 1998) and this goes beyond pointing and clicking, which, at its worst, can be a superficial, haphazard activity. Engagement requires an element of reflection on choices and their effects. It might also include prediction, trial and evaluation. The prize of interactivity is understanding, but it cannot be won without cognitive effort (Laurillard 1995, cited in Stoney and Wild 1998).

Readers are invited to reflect on the range of software uses described in earlier chapters and identify the properties and potential learning benefits implicit in each for their own use in the science classroom. The main focus in identifying properties should be on those that represent an enhancement on conventional methods. In this way the list defines the 'added value' conferred by ICT.

Skills with software

A key idea developed in this discussion is that the manner of application of software has a crucial effect on learning benefits. It then follows that, in science, for teachers and students alike, the skills needed for successful use are wider than those simply needed to operate the computer and the program; we also need to identify 'application' skills, which are required to enable software properties to deliver scientific learning benefits.

For the science teacher, an important aspect of application skill resides in the investment in task design, target setting and intervention strategies. At the planning stage, the identification of clear learning objectives for any class activity, as discussed earlier, needs to involve consideration of the mode of learning and an appreciation of the 'qualities' or 'added value' offered by potential software. For example, multimedia software on animal habitats may provide a useful source of information, but the learning value of such software depends upon how well the task prompts students to think about the relationships between the variables involved. The software itself needs to be evaluated for its suitability of content in relation to the science curriculum, its intended level of use and scope for differentiation according to students' needs; if informational software published for the general adult market is chosen, it needs to be scrutinized carefully for reading age and conceptual demands; if the learning objective lies in conceptual development, the software should support investigative activity and encourage analytical and divergent thinking.

For students, application skills need to embrace procedural understanding about the software tools concerned. For example, the use of web-sourced information requires searching, selecting and validating skills, all demanding a level of thought beyond the mere operational knowledge of the navigation tools; criteria are needed for defining productive searches, judgement is needed for making choices and validating data. With graphing software, students need to appreciate the significance of graph shape, describe the behaviour of variables, compare sets of data, make predictions, relate variables and so on. With simulations, they need a rationale for purposeful investigations, controlling variables, fair testing and so on. Successful acquisition of application skills should make it easier for students to plan their own tasks and ask their own questions with software.

Planning science activities with ICT requires a suitable balance between the demands of operational and application skills. In the context of ICT for science lessons, the list of operational skills needs to be kept as short as possible, while retaining compatibility with learning objectives. Acquiring ICT tools skills may be relatively easy, but gaining the wisdom to use them effectively is not (Ragsdale 1991; Underwood 1994), yet the latter is the key to successful learning outcomes.

The role of the science teacher

Evidence from research into the effectiveness of ICT in the classroom highlights the importance of the role of teacher (see, for example, Rogers and Wild 1996). The preceding discussion of software skills has explored some of the planning and training aspects of this role. We now turn to the management of the activity during the science lesson. Here it might be more appropriate to consider the effect that ICT has on the teacher's role, rather than the converse. In practice, the effects of the teacher and the software are mutually interdependent; the success of the ICT in science depends upon the teacher's strategy, yet the teacher's mode of working in the laboratory or classroom is affected by ICT.

In the laboratory or classroom, teachers have a variety of roles, which they learn to balance and choreograph (Loveless 1995: 20). Traditionally, these include leader, motivator, manager, knowledge provider, interpreter, adviser, prompter, quality controller, trouble-shooter, challenger and respondent. When ICT is introduced into the laboratory or classroom, most of these roles are retained but their relative importance needs to be adjusted. For example, the acquisition of knowledge through information systems on CD-ROMs and the Internet diminishes the traditional role of the teacher as a knowledge provider. For skills learning, software tutorials can manage the learning of operational aspects, leaving the teacher to focus on procedural learning. For conceptual learning, although software tools can provide excellent interactivity, it is difficult to replace the skill of the teacher as an interpreter. As a general principle, computers are at their best at facilitating learning when students work individually or in pairs (Loveless 1995: 147). It is argued that cooperative groups, facilitating discussion and sharing of learning experiences, provide the most effective class arrangements (Underwood and Underwood 1990: 168), but whole-class teaching, using the computer as a demonstration tool, often fails to exploit the interactive potential of software. Thus, with ICT, the balance of teaching and learning styles in science needs to move towards more student autonomy and less teacher direction.

With or without ICT, ceding responsibility to students is a challenge for the teacher. The mutual trust required is not built in one lesson but requires careful training of attitudes as well as skills. In recent years, science teachers in the UK have devoted considerable effort to developing investigative approaches to practical science in which students are encouraged to question, plan, design, decide, predict, observe, measure, record, draw conclusions and generally think for themselves. Rarely does this sort of student-centred activity happen without careful preparation and management by teachers. It is worth reminding ourselves of the strategies and skills experienced teachers have developed in order to achieve this method of working, because they are no less relevant when ICT is introduced into the learning situation. Teachers have good detective skills aimed at finding out what students are thinking and doing; they diagnose students' attitude and motivation, identify distractions and obstacles to understanding and articulate students' conceptual problems. Teachers empathize with students, breaking their problems down into 'manageable chunks', not always giving an immediate answer but prompting students' own thought to lead them to their own conclusions. Teachers respond to students to give encouragement and approval, to set targets, to monitor pace as well as progress and to reward effort. The teacher is a trouble-shooter in the general sense, giving advice for avoiding pitfalls, looking ahead yet reflecting on what has gone before.

It is hard to imagine a computer emulating these skills, yet they are needed as much as ever when ICT is used in a science lesson, so there will always be a role for the teacher. However, it is all too easy, when using ICT, for teachers and students to be distracted by technical issues that displace the type of interactions implied above. It is unfortunate when the teacher's attention becomes dominated by technical problems or misunderstandings; we shall have to trust that the continued efforts of designers, developers and technicians will relegate such problems as minor issues. In the meantime, science teachers should strive to employ their well-rehearsed professional skills during lessons with ICT to maximize its potential. For example, they should be seeking constructive interventions such as these:

- remind students what they have learnt already and build upon this;
- highlight the special qualities of the software techniques and suggest further examples of their useful application;
- prompt students to make *links* between observations or some other knowledge;
- help to reduce the possibility of 'early closure' of students' own discussion;
- prompt students to make a prediction and compare it with actuality;
- help to interpret the implications for science and keep the science questions to the fore.

Assessment of students' work

We will not attempt here to discuss the large range of issues related to the assessment of students' work in science, but consider the associated question: 'How does ICT affect what is assessed and how it is assessed in science?'

As a general principle, the greatest attention of assessment should focus on science learning and skills rather than on software operational skills. Clearly, with the involvement of ICT, science skills are augmented and modified by application issues; for example, in the case of graphing software as discussed previously, it was noted that the ICT simplified the plotting process for graphs but also facilitated the analysis and interpretation of graphs. If the assessment process is to recognize this change, it needs to reward the innovation and give credit to its exercise. There is a parallel here to the debate about the appropriate use of calculators in mathematics teaching; certain traditional curricular ambitions are best achieved without calculators, while new objectives are facilitated with them. Ultimately, the assessment process determines what aspects of a student's performance are valued. There is the question of how far present syllabus requirements fully reflect the advances made possible with software tools. It is natural for changes to lag behind the innovation; it is to be hoped, however, that ICT will feature more frequently as syllabuses develop.

An earlier discussion placed great emphasis on the role of application skills in enabling software to deliver learning benefits. An examination of these skills shows that they demonstrate a procedural understanding that is valuable to science. For example, the skills include relating and controlling variables, planning fair tests and comparing sets of data. In view of

148

their alignment with science process skills, these too must find a place in a scheme of assessment.

The assessment of scientific knowledge and understanding is a sophisticated business for which a variety of assessment tools have been developed over the years. With the arrival of ICT in the form of *integrated learning systems* (ILS) it is tempting to imagine that a new panacea for assessment is on offer. Such systems tend to be most effective in the domain of content knowledge but need to be scrutinized carefully to consider their effectiveness for assessing skills and the understanding of concepts. A similar caution is advised with 'drill and practice' revision and practice programs; it is necessary to examine precisely what learning objectives are tested in the software.

Finally, as students increasingly use the Internet and CD-ROM information systems, the originality of their 'written' products needs consideration. The potential for plagiarism has always been present in students' written work, but the ease of 'copy and paste' operations in software elevates the problem to a new level. The reasons for copying, however, are not always laziness. It is recognized that non-fiction texts demand a greater depth of understanding compared with narrative texts (Lewis *et al.* 1995) and that the reluctance or inability of students to engage with remodelling ideas within a text probably signals a lack of understanding of the ideas. A useful strategy for diagnosing students' understanding and militating against plagiarism is to employ a variety of methods by which students are required to rework the original text into a different form. Some suggested methods are as follows:

- Paraphrase text using a smaller number of words. For example, using the 'ash' website (www.ash.org.uk) students could be asked to read the section on 'smoking, the heart and circulation', and to construct an information leaflet to provide a brief summary including some key words.
- Highlighting the key points in text. This is a well-known activity using conventional resources such as textbooks. However, ICT provides access to a much wider range of sources; for example, descriptions of scientific discoveries in CD-ROM-based encyclopaedias
- Representing the text as a series of bullet points. When studying the Solar System students could be directed to the description of Venus; for example, in the nine planets website (www.nineplanets.org). This contains an extensive description of the planets and the student could be asked to extract key data, under a number of identified headings.
- Describing a process using boxes and flow diagrams. The use of applets (or small application programs) to provide an animated view of devices and processes was discussed in Chapter 5. One way to assess a student's understanding of the working of a device, such as an electric motor, would be to ask them to describe the process by using a series of linked

text boxes. (A good source of physics-related applets can be found at http://home.a-city.de/walter.fendt/phe/phe.htm.)

- Explaining particular terms within the text. Websites such as School Science (www.schoolscience.co.uk) provide useful content on a range of topics; for example, related to the Human Genome Project. The relevant page could be printed out and students could be asked to explain the highlighted words in the text. This activity could be followed up by asking students using the 'hot links' on the web page itself to check their answers.
- Rewriting the text in a different genre or for a different audience. The use of simulations was discussed in Chapter 6. One way to follow up this type of activity would be by the use of imaginative writing. For example, if the students had been using the States of Matter simulation they could be asked to imagine that they were a molecule and to describe their 'experiences' as the material changed state.
- Representing the text as a poster. This activity could be an alternative to the bullet point exercise discussed above in relation to information on Venus.
- Giving oral explanations to other students, working in small groups. The use of software designed to help students to analyse their diets was discussed in Chapter 7. One way to follow up this type of activity would be to ask students to make a brief presentation to others. The criteria could include providing key data about the nutrients in their diet and how they might improve that diet. As an alternative the students could be asked to use PowerPoint as part of their presentation.

When suitably employed, all these methods can prompt and enhance students' scientific thinking and provide useful feedback on their understanding.

Evaluating ICT activities in science

We are now in a position to suggest some criteria that might be used to identify a maturity of pedagogy in teaching science with ICT. The early part the discussion in this chapter attempted to draw attention to the need to identify in each type of software the special qualities that can be regarded as 'added value' compared with traditional methods of working. Care was taken to distinguish between descriptions of what can be done using software, its 'properties' and the potential learning benefits that can follow as a result of using the software. The realization of learning benefits depends upon the 'application' skills employed when using the software. Some benefits consist of enhancements of traditional practice, while others represent new ways of working. In an innovatory phase, it is natural for teachers to design activities that imitate traditional methods or experiments, but it is necessary to invest time in experimenting with software to appreciate its special qualities and the nature of application skills needed to exploit them. As experience with the technology grows, good-quality software will be recognized as that which prompts new opportunities, new ways of thinking and new ways of working. For example, in the case of data-logging software: the process of automatic measuring and recording makes the tabulation of data redundant, and students can then devote more attention to observation during the experiment; if the graph is automatically plotted on the computer screen in 'real time' it provides immediate opportunities for study and analysis; a variety of analysis tools are available for obtaining more information from the graph.

A brief examination of the range of software tools available to science education reveals an impressive array of visual aids, simulations, calculating tools, graphing tools, publishing tools and information systems. Such is the wealth of software material available to the present generation of students, it may seem an impertinence to ask 'How much effect has ICT had in actually improving children's understanding of science?' Some encouraging answers can be found in two major studies conducted in the UK during the early 1990s, the *ImpaCT* study (Watson 1993) and the *PLAIT* report (Gardner *et al.* 1994), but the findings do not reflect the effect of substantial advances in software and hardware design during the late 1990s. However, at the time of writing the initial findings of the *ImpaCT2* project are being published (Harrison *et al.* 2002), which suggests that the use of ICT in science has a measurable effect on the performance of students studying science in the secondary school. The author's view is that answers to the question will always be influenced by factors that are extrinsic to the software. ICT merely provides learning tools whose use alone cannot ensure learning any more than mere attendance at lessons can ensure examination success. Of prime importance are 'application skills', discussed earlier in this chapter. Their development is a key factor in the successful integration of ICT in teaching and, at the present time, further research is needed to inform this development. Operational skills cannot be ignored but they need to be prioritized with regard to teaching purposes and every effort must be made to keep them to a minimum, lest they predominate over application skills.

The identification of learning objectives usually springs from curriculum statements and schemes of work but it is desirable that an iterative process evolves whereby teachers' developing vision of what makes software worthwhile and notions of 'added value' inform and help to redefine learning objectives. The encouragement of this process also has to be seen as a longer-term goal of teacher training in ICT, as well as guiding curriculum reform, enabling it to embrace the full potential of ICT.

Is there any evidence that this process is occurring in science teaching? Relatively recently, there has been a large-scale ICT training programme for all teachers in England, Wales and Northern Ireland funded by the New Opportunities Fund (NOF). One of the providers of this training,

'The Science Consortium', targeted ICT use in secondary science. While the outcomes seem to be patchy, there is some evidence that providing science teachers with a starting point based on a series of lessons, which are supported by lesson plans, worksheets and related software, encourages the process of incorporating ICT into schemes of work. In some cases initially sceptical teachers would report on the success of an ICT-based lesson, but more importantly on the ways in which they would modify the approach the next time they taught the lesson. Once a whole science department sees the benefit of building on a core of ICT-based lessons then the process of integrating ICT into science teaching has begun.

New ways of working in science education

An optimistic view is that school laboratories, like classrooms, will con-tinue to be places where people meet and exchange ideas. Social inter-action, discussion and 'hands-on' activity are vital aspects of the educative process that are inadequately satisfied by the solitude of individual com-puter use. Computers should not be allowed to displace essential intel-lectual exchanges between people but should be used in ways that amplify and complement them. Thus it is important to identify and understand both the benefits and the disadvantages of individual ICT tools, so that judgements about fitness for purpose can be made at every stage of plan-ning. This chapter sets out some evaluation criteria and highlights the need to consider carefully how software is used, since this has been shown to have a strong influence on learning outcomes. The preparation of stu-dents for a task, the definition of task objectives and the nature of teacher interventions all contribute to the quality of the outcomes. These factors need to be borne in mind as we consider the possible impact of some of the innovations.

The science teaching laboratory of the future promises to provide access to an unprecedentedly wide range of resources. Many of these resources will be available through the Internet, although much standard support material will be stored on CD-ROMs and school networks. As curriculum developers and publishers embrace the new technology, these resources will be designed with compatibility in mind. An excellent example has been set by the *Advancing Physics* course (Institute of Physics 2000), which offers complementary materials: an attractive textbook for setting out the course of study and motivating students; a CD-ROM providing an enormous range of standard reference material, background readings, practice questions, teachers' notes, experiment guides and software tools; a dedicated website providing a further up-to-date resource base with links to other relevant sites on the Internet. This method of publishing exploits the particular benefits of each medium and uses them in a complementary way: the book as a constant companion for students, the CD-ROM as a cost-effective method of publishing an enormous range of reference and optional materials and the website as a source of the latest versions of information that is novel or liable to rapid change. Planning for the use of these resources will help teachers to consider the individual benefits of each medium. As discussed previously, many teachers will wish to design their own customized pathways through the electronic media to serve their own preferences, the particular needs of their students or the requirements of a particular syllabus.

The welcome trend of improving compatibility and interconnectivity between software packages invites teachers to plan a more integrated approach to their use. As software technologies borrow methods from each other, a common set of operational skills emerges. Improving facilities for exchanging data and text between different systems should encourage us not to view software tools in isolation, but to explore opportunities for the integration of data gathering, analysis, presentation and communication. For example, imagine an experiment conducted with a data logger and the result presented on a graph; at the click of a button, the graph could be inserted into a word-processed document ready for descriptive text to be added; at the click of another button, the document could be saved in hypertext format and sent via a network link to the school's network server; once stored on the server, the document may be viewed using a web browser program on any computer that happens to be logged on to the network. As wireless networking technology becomes easier to install, the idea of distributing data on a school-wide scale becomes reality. Students might despatch their classwork electronically via the network or send their homework by e-mail. Teachers might find themselves marking a set of electronic portfolios instead of exercise books; the technology for this already exists, see chapter 1.

Networking facilities are likely to multiply access to local and global information sources and facilitate new collaborative learning communities. A group of schools and colleges might collaborate in providing online study materials for joint use in their locality. Students might be able to choose from a range of distance learning courses provided by different institutions. Consortia of educationalists might establish validated 'gateways' to help schools to manage the volume and diversity of information available on the Internet. Broadcasting and media organizations promise an expanded range of 'services' through digital communications and it is certain that education will feature strongly in their plans. Indeed, the plethora of information channels promised in the digital era, via satellite, cable, terrestrial broadcasting and telephone lines, further complicates the process of choice and demands new management systems.

Such ideas are mainly dreams at this stage. For some science teachers, a lesson blighted by equipment malfunctions can perhaps become a nightmare; the ICT dream soon fades when trouble-shooting takes over from education in the classroom. It is essential that the robustness and reliability of equipment improve well beyond their present level. Most of the dreams are mainly inspired by technical feasibility, but none deserves to become reality if a proven benefit to learning cannot be identified. 'Fitness for purpose' must be the guiding principle at all times. The lure of technological gadgetry for its own sake must be avoided, especially if it becomes a distraction to learning and encourages an unhealthy pre-occupation with operational rather than learning issues. However, the nature of innovation is experimental and a vision of benefits sometimes only emerges from an iterative process involving trial and evaluation. For many teachers, early steps in applying ICT often imitate traditional methods of working, then, as confidence and experience develop through experimentation and practice, new ways of working emerge. For example, data-logging experiments can be based on traditional laboratory experiments in which students spend time recording readings and plotting a graph. However, ICT data-logging methods often greatly reduce the time needed and encourage students to explore new ways of analysing the data. Sometimes ICT methods can be blended with traditional methods to exploit the benefits of each in complementary ways. For example, students might use the computer to generate attractive text and diagrams for poster production. Sometimes an innovation demands a completely new approach compared with traditional methods. For example, access to the Internet demands skills for selecting, evaluating and validating information.

Shaping the future

ICT is transforming all aspects of society: its institutions, commerce, industry, home life and education. In education, there is a growing assumption that using computers is a 'good thing'; after all, the response of many students seems to be predominantly one of high motivation. There is, however, a certain risk that the educational rationale for ICT becomes overshadowed by the glamour and progress of the hardware and software technology. Undoubtedly, technological developments will continue to invite thinking about new opportunities for teaching and learning, but it is very much easier to engage with the new technology than to seek a deep understanding of its implications for education. It is important, therefore, that pedagogy and technology are equal partners in the development process. In particular, innovations should not be driven by technology for its own sake. As guardians of pedagogy, teachers have a significant role in shaping the use of ICT for learning. Previous chapters have demonstrated the scope of the major software tools for science teaching. The future success of ICT in science rests on the quality of thought given to its use, with a clear focus on learning outcomes.

References

Gardner, J., Morrison, H., Jarman, R., Reilly, C. and McNally, H. (1994) *Personal Portable Computers and the Curriculum*. Edinburgh: Scottish Council for Research in Education.

Gott, R. and Duggan, S. (1995) *Investigative Work in the Science Curriculum*. Buckingham: Open University Press.

Harrison, C., Comber, C., Fisher, T., Haw, K., Lewin, C., Lunzer, E., McFarlane, A., Mavers, D., Scrimshaw, P., Somekh, B. and Watling, R. (2002) *ImpaCT2: The Impact of Information and Communications Technology on Pupil Learning and Attainment*. Coventry: DfEE/BECTa.

Institute of Physics (2000) *Advancing Physics*. Bristol: IOP Publishing.

Lewis, M., Wray, D. and Rospigliosi, P. (1995) 'No copying please!' Helping children to respond to non-fiction text, *Education 3–13*, 23(1): 27–34.

Loveless, A. (1995) *The Role of IT: Practical Issues for the Primary Teacher*. London: Cassell.

Newton, L. R. and Rogers, L. T. (2001) *Teaching Science with ICT*. London: Continuum.

Ragsdale, R. (1991) Effective computing in education: teachers, tools and training, *Education and Computing*, 7: 157–66.

Rogers, L. T. and Wild, P. (1996) Data-logging: effects on practical science, *Journal of Computer Assisted Learning*, 12: 130–45.

Stoney, S. and Wild, M. (1998) Motivation and interface design: maximising learning opportunities, *Journal of Computer Assisted Learning*, 14: 40–50.

Underwood, J. D. M. (1994) *Computer Based Learning: Potential into Practice*. London: David Fulton.

Underwood, J. D. M. and Underwood, G. (1990) *Computers and Learning*. Oxford: Blackwell.

Watson, D. M. (ed.) (1993) *The Impact Report: An Evaluation of the Impact of Information Technology on Children's Achievements in Primary and Secondary Schools*. London: Kings College.

10

CLOSING REMARKS

Roy Barton

Looking back through the chapters in this book it is striking to note the variety of ways in which ICT can be employed to enhance the teaching of science. This prompted me to reflect on whether the 'nature' of science education itself means that the use of ICT is especially appropriate. This suggestion has been backed up to some extent by the findings of an *ImpaCT2* report (Harrison *et al.* 2002), which singled out science as one of the subjects in which the use of ICT seems to have had a measurable effect on pupils' performance in external tests.

To explore this proposition it is useful to look more closely at some of the key elements involved in science education. For example:

- dealing with abstract ideas and concepts;
- visualizing dynamic processes and complex interactions;
- experimentation and investigation;
- pattern finding, that is looking for the relationship between variables;
- the mathematical processing of data;
- an introduction to a large and constantly changing body of knowledge.

However, before I outline how each of these facets of science teaching can be supported by the use of ICT it is worth stressing that we are focusing on the potential of ICT to *enhance* and *improve* the effectiveness of science education, not to replace conventional approaches. Clearly, it is perfectly possible to teach science well without any use of ICT, but the question is: which aspects of the subject can benefit especially from its use?

Dealing with abstract ideas and concepts

One of the most difficult aspects of science teaching is that we often deal with abstract ideas that are difficult to explain or to demonstrate directly. As a consequence we are sometimes faced with the problem of linking pupils' concrete experience to an abstract model. Earlier in this book we have been given a number of examples of how simulations can assist in this process; for example, the ways in which simulated interactions between molecules can support the teaching of reaction rates or how the use of animations to show the movement of ions can be particularly helpful when trying to explain the processes involved in electrolysis.

Visualizing dynamic and complex interactions

The three-dimensional and dynamic nature of scientific processes and devices provides a challenge to science teachers. There are a number of examples where a simple animation, such as a moving model of an electric motor, can make all the difference when trying to explain how such devices operate. This is also the case when teaching about situations that change with time, such as the variation in the speed of a falling object. Simulations that show in real time the ways in which the forces change, and at the same time provide a graphical record of these changes, are vastly superior to any other method I have tried.

Experimentation and investigation

Practical work features prominently in most texts related to science education and this book is no exception. Unlike the examples discussed above, the use of ICT to support practical work in science is a little more contentious. Chapters 2, 3 and 4 address these concerns. However, the potential benefits of ICT for extending the range of hands-on experimental work and providing tools for pupil-directed investigatory work are well accepted. The use of ICT to support investigations is not well developed, in part due to limited resources; however, ICT offers an opportunity to provide tools to enable pupils to explore a much wider range of situations and to get access to much higher quality data. For example, investigations on the factors that affect the speed of a moving object, such as the slope of a ramp, the size of the frictional drag or the distance travelled, benefit from the ability to measure speed directly, quickly and accurately.

Pattern finding, looking for the relationship between variables

Spreadsheets and data-logging software offer tools to support the exploration of the relationship between variables, which is an important aspect of science education. The ability to use sensors to collect data for a wide range of quantities and the mathematical tools to manipulate these data are key factors here.

Mathematical processing of data

Spreadsheets in particular can provide support for pupils when processing data. Although the software tools must not be a substitute for developing pupils' numeracy skills, they can be effective in getting pupils to focus on the science content rather than getting 'bogged down' in processing. Chapter 7 provides a number of examples to illustrate how this can be done in practice.

An introduction to a large and constantly changing body of knowledge

In the past the main source of information in the science laboratory, other than the teacher, has been the science textbook, which is generally effective for the well-established parts of the science curriculum but less useful for recent developments. The use of the Internet as a tool for pupil exploration or as a background resource for the teacher can change this situation. We should not underestimate the motivating power of finding out about recent developments or information about the earthquake that struck only yesterday. If such information can give pupils more of a sense of the human struggle associated with scientific advances and the excitement related to pushing back the frontiers of our scientific knowledge, then perhaps this will go some way towards changing pupils' perceptions of science as an unchanging body of knowledge.

From consideration of these closing remarks and looking at the discussions in the book as a whole, it is apparent that ICT has the *potential* to make an enormous impact on science teaching and learning. However, for a number of reasons, related to, for example, resources, training, time and lack of experience, it is fair to say that the full potential of ICT in science education has yet to be realized.

It is the hope of all those involved in the production of this book that we will have made some contribution towards developing this potential a little further.

Reference

Harrison, C., Comber, C., Fisher, T., Haw, K., Lewin, C., Lunzer, E., McFarlane, A., Mavers, D., Scrimshaw, P., Somekh, B. and Watting, R. (2002) *ImpaCT2. The Impact of Information and Communications Technology on Pupil Learning and Attainment*. Coventry: DfES/BECTa.

INDEX

abstract ideas, 156
applet, 75
assessment, 57, 62, 125, 147–9

case studies
  burning candle, 46
  cost of electrical energy, 123
  electrical characteristics, 63
  energy stored in food, 112
  energy transfer, 34
  evaporation, 29
  multimedia motion, 90
  pollution and aquatic invertebrates,
    58
  rates of reaction, 49
  reaction time, 116
  stopping distance, 53
Coach software, 131
  resonance project, 134
communication, 12
concepts, 140

database
  diet analyser, 110

elements, 115
data logging hardware
  equipment, 40, 44
  sensors, 40–2
data logging software
  analysing tools, 36, 49, 91
  curve fitting, 54
  real time, 41
  remote, 36, 41, 62
  set-up files, 65
  snapshot, 58
data projector, 45

e-mail, 84

graph
  analysis, 31
  computer-aided, 32, 143
  manual, 31–2
  sketch, 33, 38, 46, 66

health and safety, 36, 76
hyperlinks,, 9
hypothesis testing, 116

ImpaCT2 study, 150, 155
Integrated Learning System (ILS),
    148
interactivity, 92, 102, 119, 144
Internet
  directories, 78
  KennisNet, 131
  off-line, 75
  publishing, 82
  resources, 72
  search engine, 79
  solar system, 73

literacy, 14

Mimio, 19
modelling, 119–23, 133
motivation, 13, 96, 112, 153
multimedia
  added value, 94
  dangerous experiments, 93
  misrepresentation, 98

numeracy, 13

practical work
  aims, 28
  circus, 48
  demonstration, 33,, 46
  fieldwork, 58

investigation, 53, 108, 146
  whole-class, 50

scroll bars, 13
simulations, 16,, 75
software,
  evaluating, 99
  properties, 142
spreadsheet
  generic, 109
  investigation, 124
  patterns in data, 113
  template, 112
studyhouse, 130
science skills, 141

teachers, role of, 29, 37, 57, 66, 145
technical support, 27
training, 27, 45

video camera, 24
video-conferencing, 19, 85
virtual
  laboratory, 92
  learning, 17
  microscope, 89
  walk, 89
visualising science, 156

wireless/radio network, 23, 152

LANGUAGE AND LITERACY IN SCIENCE EDUCATION

Jerry Wellington and Jonathan Osborne

All teachers look and hope for more scientific forms of expression and reasoning from their pupils, but few have been taught specific techniques for supporting students' use of scientific language. This book is full of them . . . In this very practical book, Jerry Wellington and Jonathan Osborne do much more than summarize research which shows how very much language, in all its forms, matters to science education. They also show teachers what can be done to make learning science through language both more effective and more enjoyable.

Jay L. Lemke, Professor of Education, City University of New York

Science in secondary schools has tended to be viewed mainly as a 'practical subject', and language and literacy in science education have been neglected. But learning the language of science is a major part of science education: every science lesson is a language lesson, and language is a major barrier to most school students in learning science. This accessible book explores the main difficulties in the language of science and examines practical ways to aid students in retaining, understanding, reading, speaking and writing scientific language.

Jerry Wellington and Jonathan Osborne draw together and synthesize current good practice, thinking and research in this field. They use many practical examples, illustrations and tried-and-tested materials to exemplify principles and to provide guidelines in developing language and literacy in the learning of science. They also consider the impact that the growing use of information and communications technology has had, and will have, on writing, reading and information handling in science lessons.

The authors argue that paying more attention to language in science classrooms is one of the most important acts in improving the quality of science education. This is a significant and very readable book for all student and practising secondary school science teachers, for science advisers and school mentors.

Contents
Acknowledgements – Introduction: the importance of language in science education – Looking at the language of science – Talk of the classroom: language interactions between teachers and pupils – Learning from reading – Writing for learning in science – Discussion in school science: learning science through talking – Writing text for learning science – Practical ploys for the classroom – Last thoughts . . . – References – Appendix – Index.

160pp   0 335 20598 4 (Paperback)   0 335 20599 2 (Hardback)

MEANING MAKING IN SECONDARY SCIENCE CLASSROOMS

Eduardo Mortimer and Philip Scott

This book focuses on the talk of science classrooms and in particular on the ways in which the different kinds of interactions between teachers and students contribute to meaning making and learning. Central to the text is a new analytical framework for characterising the key features of the talk of school science classrooms. This framework is based on sociocultural principles and links the work of theorists such as Vygotsky and Bakhtin to the day-to-day interactions of contemporary science classrooms. The book:

- Provides detailed examples and illustrations of insights gained from applying the framework to real science lessons in the UK and Brazil;
- Demonstrates how these ways of thinking about classroom talk can be drawn upon to inform the professional development of science teachers;
- Offers an innovative research methodology, based on sociocultural theory, for analysing classroom talk.

This book offers a powerful set of tools for thinking and talking about the day-to-day practices of contemporary science classrooms. It contains messages of fundamental importance and insight for all of those who are interested in reflecting on the interactions of science teaching and learning, whether in the context of teaching, higher degree study, or research.

Contents

Foreword by James V. Wertsch – Doing and talking school science – Teaching science, learning science – Capturing and characterising the talk of school science – From everyday to scientific ideas: a teaching and learning performance – Struggling to come to terms with the scientific story – Looking back . . . looking forward – Appendix – Bibliography – Index.

160pp   0 335 21207 7 (Paperback)   0 335 21208 5 (Hardback)

GOOD PRACTICE IN SCIENCE TEACHING
WHAT RESEARCH HAS TO SAY
Martin Monk and Jonathan Osborne (eds)

This book offers a summary of major educational research and scholarship important to the field of science education. Written, in a clear, concise and readable style, the authors have identified the principal messages and their implications for the practice of science teaching. Aimed at science teachers of children of all ages, and others who work in teaching and related fields, the book provides an invaluable first guide for science teachers. All of the chapters are written by authors from King's College and the University of Leeds, both of which are institutions with an international reputation for their work in the field with top research ratings. Each chapter summarizes the research work and evidence in the field, discussing its significance, reliability and implications. Valuable lists of further reading and full references are provided at the end of each chapter.

Contents
Introduction – Part one: The science classroom – Strategies for learning – Formative assessment – Children's thinking, learning, teaching and constructivism – The role of practical work – The nature of scientific knowledge – The role of language in the learning and teaching of science – Students' attitudes towards science – Part two: The science department – Managing the science department – Summative assessment – Science teaching and the development of intelligence – Progression and differentiation – Information and communications technologies: their role and value for science education – Part three: The science world – GNVQ Science at Advanced level: a new kind of course – Science for citizenship – Index.

256pp   0 335 20391 4 (Paperback)   0 335 20392 2 (Hardback)